21. 15
1.8 P

D0205387

FREE
MONEY®
FOR
COLLEGE

5th EDITION

ALSO BY LAURIE BLUM

BUSINESS

FREE MONEY® FOR SMALL BUSINESSES & ENTREPRENEURS	(John Wiley)
FREE MONEY® WHEN YOU'RE UNEMPLOYED	(John Wiley)
FREE MONEY® FROM THE FEDERAL GOVERNMENT	
FOR SMALL BUSINESSES AND ENTREPRENEURS	(John Wiley)

EDUCATION

FREE MONEY® FOR COLLEGE	(Facts On File)
FREE MONEY® FOR GRADUATE SCHOOL	(Facts On File)
FREE MONEY® FOR FOREIGN STUDY	(Facts On File)

HEALTH CARE

FREE MONEY® FOR SENIORS AND THEIR FAMILIES	(John Wiley)

OTHER

THE COMPLETE GUIDE TO GETTING A GRANT	(John Wiley)
FREE DOLLARS FROM THE FEDERAL GOVERNMENT	(John Wiley)

FREE MONEY® FOR COLLEGE

5th EDITION

LAURIE BLUM

Facts On File, Inc.

FREE MONEY® FOR COLLEGE, 5th Edition

Copyright © 1999 by Laurie Blum

Checkmark Books
An imprint of Facts On File, Inc.
11 Penn Plaza
New York NY 10001

Library of Congress Cataloging-in-Publication Data
Blum, Laurie.
Free money for college / Laurie Blum.—5th ed.
p.   cm.
Includes bibliographical references (p.   ) and index.
ISBN 0-8160-3947-X.—ISBN 0-8160-3948-8 (pbk. : alk. paper)
1. Student aid—United States—Directories. 2. Scholarships—United States—Directories.
I. Title.
LB2337.2.B57 1998
378.3'02573—dc21 98-39651

You can find Facts On File on the World Wide Web at
http://www.factsonfile.com

Text design by Evelyn Horovicz
Cover design by Cathy Rincon

Printed in the United States of America

MP FOF 10 9 8 7 6 5 4 3 2 1
   (pbk) 10 9 8 7 6 5 4 3 2 1

This book is printed on acid-free paper.

CONTENTS

INTRODUCTION / vii

STATE LISTINGS / 1

AREA OF STUDY LISTINGS / 169

MISCELLANEOUS LISTINGS / 191

GRANTS FOR WOMEN / 195

GRANTS FOR ETHNIC STUDENTS / 197

GRANTS FOR DISABLED STUDENTS / 203

BIBLIOGRAPHY / 207

INDEX / 209

INTRODUCTION

Would you like to have enough money to attend any college or university you want, regardless of how much it costs?

How many impoverished or would-be students have not applied for financial aid because they decided in advance that they had no chance of success?

There really is approximately three billion dollars given away *free* to students each year. There are also low-cost loans and many other ways that mean that yes, you *can* afford to go to school. Many of these sources fund students regardless of their financial need or academic excellence.

Do you just walk up, hold out your hand, and expect someone to put money in it? Of course not. It takes time, effort, and thought on your part. You're going to have to find out who is giving away money. You're going to have to fill out applications. You may meet with frustration or rejection somewhere down the road. The odds, however, are in your favor that you will qualify for some sort of financial aid.

The hardest part has always been finding the sources of money, which is why I wrote this book. This book provides you, the reader, with the actual sources of monies available.

In this country tens of thousands of foundations give grants, an impossible number for anyone to wade through—nor is there any reason why you should. For this book, I've listed the scholarships and grants that apply to as many undergraduate students as possible.

The listings are divided into four categories to make this book as easy to use as possible. Check all four categories to see which grants apply to you. The geographic listings apply to where you live and in many cases where you go to college. Subject listings apply for the most part to your major or intended field of study. Special groups pertain to funding sources available to women, ethnic groups (such as Afro-American, Hispanic, American Indian, and Asian, as well as those with other specific religious and ancestral backgrounds), and the handicapped. The miscellaneous section includes grants available to members of fraternal organizations, those with specific hobbies or interests, as well as grants with no geographic, area of study, or special group restrictions. Regardless of your field of study or your geographic location, you should qualify for at least some of the grants in this book.

I have included wherever possible the total amount of money that is awarded to students, the number of scholarships or grants given, the average size of an award, and the range of monies given. Do not be dissuaded from applying if the average award is only $200 (the same material you put together for one application can be used for most, if not all, of the other applications; you will hopefully apply for a number of scholarships and grants). You might get more, you might get less. But remember, this is free money!

HOW TO APPLY

Applying for grants and scholarships is a lot like applying for school: it takes work, thought, and organization. But at this stage in your life, you know what you have to do. You've done it before.

First comes the sorting out process. Go through this book and mark off all the listings that could give you money. Pay close attention to the restrictions and eliminate the least likely foundations. The effort you'll have to put in will probably limit you to no more than eight applications (if you are ambitious and want to apply to more than eight foundations, bravo, go right ahead). Write or call the most likely foundations to get a copy of their guidelines. (In cases where the contact's name is not listed, begin your letter: To Whom It May Concern). If you call, just request the guidelines; don't interrogate the poor person who answers the phone!

Grant applications, like college applications, take time to fill out. Often you will be required to write one or more essays. Be neat! You may very well prepare a top-notch proposal, but it won't look good if it's done in a sloppy manner. Proposals should always be typed, double-spaced, and be *sure* to make a copy of the proposal. I've learned the hard way that there is nothing worse than having the foundation not be able to find your proposal and having to reconstruct it because you didn't keep a copy. Many applications will require any previous college transcripts. Often the tax returns of both the applicant (if you had filed a return the previous year) and your parents are needed. Sometimes an interview is required (you probably had some interviews when you were looking at colleges, right?). You may be asked to include personal references (be sure to notify the people you are planning to use as references; there is nothing worse than having a foundation contact your reference, who has no idea what it is about). Remember, you have to sell yourself and convince the grantors to give money to *you* and not to someone else.

FEDERAL MONEY

Historically, federal aid has been a mainstay for the student seeking money for college. It remains one of the first sources of money you should pursue. Apply for financial aid. The process is not complicated, but you must fill out the applications to be considered. It is well worth your time and effort to explore the resources available to you. Approximately $50 billion is available in student aid. The U.S. Department of Education offers six main student aid programs, some of which are grants that do not have to be paid back; others are loans that must be paid back with interest. These programs include Pell grants, Federal Supplemental Educational Opportunity Grants (FSEOG), Federal Work-Study (FWS), Federal Perkins loans, Federal Stafford loans, and Federal Direct loans.

Federal Pell grants provide help to undergraduate students and do not have to be paid back. The maximum award is $2,700 per year. The amount you receive is based on your financial need, on whether you are a full-time or part-time student, and on the cost of your tuition, food, housing, books, and supplies.

Federal Supplemental Educational Opportunity Grants, like Pell grants, are available to undergraduate students to help pay for their college education. This money does not have to be repaid. You can receive a maximum of $4,000 a year depending on your financial need, the availability of FSEOG funds at your school, the total cost of your education, and the amount of other financial aid you are receiving. This grant is for students with exceptional financial need; priority is given to Pell grant recipients.

Federal Work-Study. Under this program, each year the federal government grants funds to colleges so that they can pay students who have financial need. Your pay will be at least the current minimum wage.

Federal Perkins loans are loans, not grants. The maximum amount of loans offered is $3,000 a year for up to five years of undergraduate study. The interest rate is 5%. This loan is for students with exceptional financial need; they may take up to 10 years to repay the loan.

Federal Stafford loans are low-interest loans made by a lender such as a bank, a savings and loan association, or a credit union. The interest rate varies annually (up to a maximum of 8.25%). The maximum amount dependent students may borrow in any one year is $2,625 for freshmen, $3,500 for sophomores, and $5,500 for juniors and seniors, with a maximum of $23,000 as an undergraduate. The maximum amount independent students can borrow is $6,625 for freshmen (no more than $2,625 in subsidized Stafford loans), $7,500 for sophomores (no more than $3,500 in subsidized Stafford loans), and $10,500 for juniors and seniors (no more than $5,500 in subsidized Stafford loans). Borrowers must pay a 4% fee, which is deducted from the loan proceeds.

Federal Plus loans. Federal Plus loans are loans that parents borrow for their children. Like Stafford loans, Federal Plus loans are made by a lender, such as a bank, credit union, or savings and loan association. Plus loans have a variable interest rate, adjusted each year that cannot exceed 9%. Repayment begins sixty days after the money is loaned. A 4% fee is subtracted from the proceeds. Parent borrowers must generally have a good credit record to qualify for Federal Plus.

Federal Direct Student loans. The Federal Direct Student loan is a relatively new program that is similar to the Federal Stafford. The difference is that the U.S. Department of Education is the lender rather than a bank. Not all colleges participate in this program, and if your child's college does not, he or she can still apply for a Federal Stafford loan. Students have a choice of repayment plans. They may choose either a fixed monthly payment for ten years; a different fixed monthly payment for twelve to thirty years at a rate that varies with the loan balance; or a variable monthly payment for up to twenty-five years that is based on a percentage of income. Students cannot receive both a Federal Direct Student loan and a Federal Stafford loan for the same period of time, but may receive both in different enrollment periods.

OTHER SOURCES OF MONEY

Although you have probably been told this many times, you should check with the various organizations you belong to (Boy Scouts, fraternities, etc.), places of worship you attend, and employers your parents or you have worked for. Thousands of corporations have programs that pay for all or part of their employees' or children of employees' school expenses. There is an enormous number of unused employee tuition benefits. Your hobbies or talents may qualify you for prizes or awards. If you are a veteran or the child of a veteran, you probably qualify for some scholarship money.

Many millions of dollars in athletic scholarships go unclaimed each year simply because no one applied for them, or because the athletic departments couldn't find enough qualified applicants.

Before you reject this category because you are not a 250-pound left tackle or do not have the backhand of Monica Seles, consider the following.

Until the late 1970s it was all too common for colleges to have multi-million-dollar training facilities for the football and basketball teams, while the women's volleyball team practiced on a muddy lot with a clothesline stretched between two poles. A law that took effect in 1978 decreed that schools must provide male and female athletes with "equal benefits and opportunities." That means separate but equal practice facilities, equipment, number of coaches, number of games, *and* scholarship money.

In the late 1970s and early 1980s the sports pages were filled with tales of academic abuses committed by outstanding athletes. There are now restrictions on how poorly the star quarterback can do academically before he is asked to leave school. One of the results of these scandals is the limit imposed by a school on how many scholarships can be awarded in the "major" sports (football, basketball, track and field, softball), with requirements that money be distributed among women athletes in these sports, as well as in archery, badminton, bowling, crew, and handball.

Schools are not restricted in how they spend their recruiting time and effort, only their scholarship money. Consequently, they will often devote a considerable amount of time and effort seeking out the best basketball and football players, but pay little or no attention to seeking out the best archery, bowling, or lacrosse athletes. If someone happens to turn up and ask for scholarship money, fine. If not, the money goes back into the general fund. No big deal. *Wide World of Sports* hasn't yet paid a dime for the rights to collegiate riflery! So be sure not to neglect some of your less obvious skills; one of them might help pay for your college education.

Finally, be sure to request information from your high school guidance counselor and the financial aid office at each school you have applied to. They can explain what scholarships or other forms of aid the university offers.

Paying for college isn't a one-year, one-shot deal. You must think in terms of this year's costs, next year's costs, and the following year's costs. If tuition charges strain you now, how desperate are you going to be by the time you are a junior?

ONE FINAL NOTE

By the time this book is published, some of the information contained here will have changed. No reference book can be as up to date as the reader or author would like. Names, addresses, dollar amounts, telephone numbers, and other data are always in flux; however, most of the information will not have changed.

Good luck.

FREE
MONEY®
FOR
COLLEGE

5th EDITION

STATE LISTINGS

ALABAMA

ALABAMA GI DEPENDENTS' SCHOLARSHIP PROGRAM
DEPARTMENT OF VETERANS AFFAIRS
P.O. Box 1509
Montgomery, AL 36102-1509

Restrictions: Children under 26 or spouses or widows of veterans who were prisoners of war, disabled, or missing in action
$ Given: Full scholarships

FFA WAL-MART SCHOLARSHIP
P.O. Box 15160
Alexandria, VA 22309-0160
(703) 360-3600

Restrictions: FFA member; freshman-year agriculture major; resident of Alabama, Arkansas, Arizona, California, Colorado, Connecticut, Delaware, Florida, Georgia, Hawaii, Idaho, Illinois, Indiana, Iowa, Kansas, Kentucky, Louisiana, Maine, Maryland, Michigan, Minnesota, Mississippi, Missouri, Montana, Nebraska, Nevada, New Hampshire, New Mexico, New York, North Carolina, North Dakota, Ohio, Oklahoma, Oregon, Pennsylvania, Puerto Rico, Rhode Island, South Carolina, South Dakota, Tennessee, Texas, Utah, Virginia, Washington State, West Virginia, Wisconsin, or Wyoming
$ Given: Approximately 50 awards of $1,000
   Deadline: February 15

GIBSON FOUNDATION
P.O. Box 311046
Enterprise, AL 36331
(334) 393-4553

Restrictions: Residents of Coffee County, AL, for health-related study
$ Given: 35 grants, $100–$1,000

JAMES M. HOFFMAN SCHOLARSHIP TRUST

c/o South Trust Bank of Alabama, N.A.
P.O. Box 1000
Anniston, AL 36202
(205) 238-1000

Contact: Bill Priddy
Restrictions: Graduate of high school in Calhoun County, AL only.
Referral by high school guidance counselor
$ Given: Unavailable
  Deadline: March 31

NUCOR FOUNDATION, INC.

2100 Rexford Road
Charlotte, NC 28211
(704) 366-7000

Contacts: Elizabeth Wells
Restrictions: Children of Nucor employees only; must maintain
2.0 GPA in college
$ Given: Up to $2,200 per year for four years
  Deadline: March 1

THE SIMPSON FOUNDATION

c/o Regions Bank
P.O. Box 511
Montgomery, AL 36101-0511
(334) 832-8200

Contact: Brock Holt
Restrictions: Residents of Wilcox County, AL
$ Given: Average $1,000–$2,000
  Deadline: March 1

JOHN W. WILL JOURNALISM SCHOLARSHIP

Mobile Chapter of the Society of Professional Journalists
P.O. Box 290
Mobile, AL 36601-0290

Contact: William Steele Holman II

Restrictions: Alabama resident with an interest in writing
$ Given: $3,500
   Deadline: March 22

ALASKA

GOLDSTEIN SCOTTISH RITE TRUST
P.O. Box 021194
Juneau, AK 99802

Contact: James H. Taylor, Manager
4365 North Douglas Road
Juneau, AK 99801
(907) 586-2849

Restrictions: Needy graduates of local Juneau, AK, high schools only
$ Given: Varies
   Deadline: April 1

STATE EDUCATIONAL INCENTIVE GRANT PROGRAM
Alaska Commission on Postsecondary Education
3030 Vintage Boulevard
Juneau, AK 99801-7109

Restrictions: Alaska residents with substantial financial need who maintain a satisfactory grade point average
$ Given: Awards range up to $1,500 per year
   Deadline: May 31

ROBERT C. THOMAS MEMORIAL SCHOLARSHIP LOAN FUND
Department of Education
801 West 10th Street
Suite 200
Juneau, AK 99801-1894

Restrictions: Students wishing to pursue a degree program leading to a

career in education, public administration, or other closely related fields
$ Given: Loans up to $1,000 per year. Upon degree completion, the
recipient receives forgiveness of 20 percent of the total loan indebtedness
for each year of full-time employment in education or public administration in Alaska
Deadline: March 1

ARIZONA

FFA WAL-MART SCHOLARSHIP
P.O. Box 15160
Alexandria, VA 22309-0160
(703) 360-3600

Restrictions: FFA member; freshman-year agriculture major; resident of
Alabama, Arkansas, Arizona, California, Colorado, Connecticut,
Delaware, Florida, Georgia, Hawaii, Idaho, Illinois, Indiana, Iowa, Kansas,
Kentucky, Louisiana, Maine, Maryland, Michigan, Minnesota, Mississippi,
Missouri, Montana, Nebraska, Nevada, New Hampshire, New Mexico,
New York, North Carolina, North Dakota, Ohio, Oklahoma, Oregon,
Pennsylvania, Puerto Rico, Rhode Island, South Carolina, South Dakota,
Tennessee, Texas, Utah, Virginia, Washington State, West Virginia, Wisconsin, or Wyoming
$ Given: Approximately 50 awards of $1,000
Deadline: February 15

NUCOR FOUNDATION, INC.
2100 Rexford Road
Charlotte, NC 28211
(704) 366-7000

Contact: Elizabeth Wells
Restrictions: Children of Nucor employees only; must maintain
2.0 GPA in college
$ Given: Up to $2,200 per year for four years
Deadline: March 1

ARKANSAS

ARKANSAS SINGLE PARENT SCHOLARSHIPS

614 East Emma
Suite 119
Springdale, AR 72764
(501) 927-1402

Contact: Ralph H. Nesson, Director
Restrictions: Arkansas residents who are single parents; need based
$ Given: Approximately 300–500 awards, range $100–$500

ARKANSAS STUDENT ASSISTANCE GRANT PROGRAM

Arkansas Department of Higher Education
114 East Capitol
Little Rock, AR 72201-3818
(501) 682-4475

Contact: Financial Aid Coordinator
Restrictions: Arkansas high school seniors who have a minimum 2.5 GPA and financial need
$ Given: Awards range up to $1,500 and are renewable for up to three additional years

FFA WAL-MART SCHOLARSHIP

P.O. Box 15160
Alexandria, VA 22309-0160
(703) 360-3600

Restrictions: FFA member; freshman-year agriculture major; resident of Alabama, Arkansas, Arizona, California, Colorado, Connecticut, Delaware, Florida, Georgia, Hawaii, Idaho, Illinois, Indiana, Iowa, Kansas, Kentucky, Louisiana, Maine, Maryland, Michigan, Minnesota, Mississippi, Missouri, Montana, Nebraska, Nevada, New Hampshire, New Mexico, New York, North Carolina, North Dakota, Ohio, Oklahoma, Oregon, Pennsylvania, Puerto Rico, Rhode Island, South Carolina, South Dakota, Tennessee, Texas, Utah, Virginia, Washington State, West Virginia, Wisconsin, or Wyoming
$ Given: Approximately 50 awards of $1,000
Deadline: February 15

GOVERNOR'S SCHOLARS
Arkansas Department of Higher Education
114 East Capitol
Little Rock, AR 72201-3818
(501) 682-4475

Contact: Financial Aid Division
Restrictions: Arkansas high school seniors who have a minimum
3.6 GPA
$ Given: $4,000 per year for four years
    Deadline: March 1

ED E. AND GLADYS HURLEY FOUNDATION
Bank One
P.O. Box 21116
Shreveport, LA 71154
(318) 226-2110

Contact: Monette Holler
Restrictions: Loans to residents of Arizona, Louisiana, and Texas to
attend institution of their choice
$ Loaned: Unavailable
    Deadline: May 31

THE HARVEY AND BERNICE JONES FOUNDATION
P.O. Drawer H
Springdale, AR 72765
(501) 756-0611

Contact: Bernice Jones
Restrictions: Primarily Springdale residents showing financial need who
plan to pursue a health-care career
$ Given: Average, $500–$1,000
    Deadline: November 30

PACIFIC PRINTING AND IMAGING ASSOCIATION
Educational Trust Scholarships
180 Nickerson, Suite 102
Seattle, WA 98109

Contact: Jim Olsen

Restrictions: Students studying printing, print management, or graphic arts technology. Must live in Washington, Oregon, Arkansas, Idaho, Montana, or Hawaii.
$ Given: 12 awards range, $500–$2,500; renewable
  Deadline: April 1

POTLATCH FOUNDATION FOR HIGHER EDUCATION SCHOLARSHIP

P.O. Box 193591
San Francisco, CA 94119-3591
(415) 576-8829

Contact: Jenni Rogers
Restrictions: Must live or attend high school within 30 miles of a major Potlatch facility; academic achievement; financial need; leadership ability
$ Given: Approximately 80 awards of $1,400
  Deadline: February 15

CALIFORNIA

ALMANOR SCHOLARSHIP FUND

c/o Collins Pine Co.
P.O. Box 796
Chester, CA 96020
(530) 258-2111

Contact: Aletha O'Kelley
Restrictions: Chester high school graduates
$ Given: Unspecified number of $1,800 and $2,400 awards
  Deadline: August 1

BORREGO SPRINGS EDUCATIONAL SCHOLARSHIP COMMITTEE

P.O. Box 59
Borrego Springs, CA 92004
(760) 767-5314

Restrictions: Borrego Springs high school graduates
$ Given: Unspecified number; maximum $1,500
  Deadline: June 30

CAL GRANT 4

P.O. Box 510845
Sacramento, CA 94245-0845
(916) 445-0880

Restrictions: California resident attending a California school; financial need
$ Given: Average award $2,500; approximately 39,000 awards given each year
    Deadline: March 2

CAL STATE B

P.O. Box 510845
Sacramento, CA 94245-0845
(916) 322-5112

Restrictions: California residents attending California schools; financial need, academic excellence, disadvantaged background increases likelihood of receiving award.
$ Given: Approximately 31,000 awards averaging $1,600
    Deadline: March 2

CALIFORNIA STUDENT AID COMMISSION

Cal Grant "C" Program
P.O. Box 510845
Sacramento, CA 94245-0845
(916) 322-2807

Restrictions: California residents for minimum 12 months; undergraduates to study occupational, technical, or vocational education, or nursing; financial need; U.S. citizens. Course length between 4 and 24 months
$ Given: 1,570 grants; range, $530–$2,360
    Deadline: March 2

CALIFORNIA TEACHERS ASSOCIATION

1705 Murchison Drive
P.O. Box 921
Burlingame, CA 94011-0921

Restrictions: California resident, member or dependent child of an active, retired, or deceased member of the California Teachers Association

$ Given: 20 $2,000 awards
   Deadline: February 15

VIVIENNE CAMP SCHOLARSHIP
Jewish Family and Children's Services
1600 Scott Street
San Francisco, CA 94115
(415) 567-8860

Restrictions: Jewish students living in the San Francisco Bay area; merit and financial need
$ Given: Four awards for $5,000 each
   Deadline: None

THE CORTI FAMILY AGRICULTURAL FUND
c/o Wells Fargo Bank, Trust Department
5262 North Blackstone
Fresno, CA 93170
(209) 442-6232

Contact: William F. Richey, Assistant Vice President, Trust, Wells Fargo Bank

Restrictions: Kern County, CA, high school graduates studying agriculture
$ Given: 133 grants totaling $24,605
   Deadline: February 28

THE EBELL OF L.A. SCHOLARSHIP ENDOWMENT FUND, AND THE MRS. CHARLES N. FLINT SCHOLARSHIP ENDOWMENT FUND
743 South Lucerne Boulevard
Los Angeles, CA 90005
(213) 931-1277

Contact: Scholarship Chairman
Restrictions: Sophomores, juniors, or seniors attending school in Los Angeles County and residents of L.A. County; must have at least 3.2 GPA
$ Given: Unspecified number of grants, each grant $300/mo. for a 10-month school year
   Deadline: May 1

FFA WAL-MART SCHOLARSHIP
P.O. Box 15160
Alexandria, VA 22309-0160
(703) 360-3600

Restrictions: FFA member; freshman-year agriculture major; resident of Alabama, Arkansas, Arizona, California, Colorado, Connecticut, Delaware, Florida, Georgia, Hawaii, Idaho, Illinois, Indiana, Iowa, Kansas, Kentucky, Louisiana, Maine, Maryland, Michigan, Minnesota, Mississippi, Missouri, Montana, Nebraska, Nevada, New Hampshire, New Mexico, New York, North Carolina, North Dakota, Ohio, Oklahoma, Oregon, Pennsylvania, Puerto Rico, Rhode Island, South Carolina, South Dakota, Tennessee, Texas, Utah, Virginia, Washington State, West Virginia, Wisconsin, or Wyoming
$ Given: Approximately 50 awards of $1,000
   Deadline: February 15

GOLDEN GATE RESTAURANT ASSOCIATION
720 Market Street, Suite 200
San Francisco, CA 94102
(415) 781-5348

Contact: Noah Froio
Restrictions: Students majoring in hotel management or culinary arts
$ Given: 15 to 20 grants totaling $30,000; average award $1,000–$1,500
   Deadline: March 31

GOLDEN STATE MINORITY FOUNDATION SCHOLARSHIP
1055 Wilshire Boulevard
Los Angeles, CA 90017
(800) 666-4763

Contact: Ivan A. Houston, President
Restrictions: Must be resident or attend school in California, Michigan, or Houston, Texas; African-American, Latino, or Native American; must be enrolled full-time, employed no more than 25 hours per week, have a minimum 3.0 GPA, and major in economics or busines administration.
$ Given: 100 $2,000 awards
   Deadlines: November 1 (Northern California, Houston); April 1 (Southern California); March 1 (Michigan)

GRAHAM-FANCHER SCHOLARSHIP FUND
149 Josephine Street, Suite A
Santa Cruz, CA 95060
(408) 423-3640

Contact: Robert H. Darrow, Trustee
Restrictions: Resident of northern Santa Cruz County, CA; graduating from high school in same area
$ Given: Seven grants, range, $100–$500
   Deadline: Apply between April 15 and May 15

FANNIE & JOHN HERTZ FOUNDATION
Box 5032
Livermore, CA 94551-5032
(510) 373-1642

Contact: Dr. Wilson K. Talley, President
Restrictions: Fellowships for graduate study in the applied physical sciences; U.S. citizens only
$ Given: $25,000 plus up to $15,000 per year cost-of-living stipend
   Deadline: October 23

THE HUMBOLDT AREA FOUNDATION
P.O. Box 99
Bayside, CA 95524
(707) 442-2993

Contact: Peter H. Pennekamp, Executive Director
Restrictions: Residents of Humboldt County, CA
$ Given: 75 grants, range, $100–$2,000
   Deadlines: April 30, May 30

OAKLAND SCOTTISH RITE
SCHOLARSHIP FOUNDATION
1547 Lakeside Drive
Oakland, CA 94612
(510) 451-1906, (510) 276-1736

Contact: Mrs. Hawkins, Secretary
Restrictions: Northern California public high school graduates chosen by the high school's financial aid office

$ Given: 200 grants of $4,000 each, renewable up to four years
   Deadline: March 17

PACIFIC GAS AND ELECTRIC COMPANY
James B. Black Scholarship
77 Beale Street
Room 2825-F
San Francisco, CA 94106
(415) 973-1338

Contact: High school guidance counselor
Restrictions: California residents living or attending school in Pacific Gas and Electric Company service area; based on SAT scores, class rank, community involvement, and job experience
$ Given: Six awards of $1,000; 12 awards of $2,000; 18 awards of $4,000
   Deadline: November 15

MARY K. AND EDITH PILLSBURY FOUNDATION
c/o Santa Barbara Foundation
15 East Carrillo Street
Santa Barbara, CA 93101
(805) 963-1873

Contact: Dan Oh, Student Aid Director
Restrictions: U.S. citizens residing in Santa Barbara County, CA, for two years prior to application. Grants are given to those who demonstrate unusual aptitude for writing and music for study in the U.S. Interviews and auditions required.
$ Given: 950 grants totaling $1.7 million; range, $400–$5,000
   Deadlines October 31 (writing); May 15 (music)

POTLATCH FOUNDATION
FOR HIGHER EDUCATION SCHOLARSHIP
P.O. Box 193591
San Francisco, CA 94119-3591
(415) 576-8829

Contact: Jenni Rogers

Restrictions: Must live or attend high school within 30 miles of a major Potlatch facility; academic achievement; financial need; leadership ability
$ Given: Approximately 80 awards of $1,400
   Deadline: February 15

CHARLES E. SAAK TRUST

c/o Wells Fargo Bank, Trust Department
8405 North Fresno Street, Suite 210
Fresno, CA 93720
(209) 442-6232

Contact: Don Compton
Restrictions: Underprivileged students under 21 years of age residing in the Porterville/Poplar area of Tulare County, CA
$ Given: Range, $90–$500
   Deadline: March 31

SCHOLARSHIP FOUNDATION OF SANTA BARBARA

P.O. Box 1403
Santa Barbara, CA 93102
(805) 965-7212

Contact: Colette Hadley, Student Aid Director
Restrictions: Graduates of Santa Barbara high schools; financial need and motivation
$ Given: 600 grants annually; range, $1,000–$2,500
   Deadline: February 1

STEPHENSON SCHOLARSHIP FOUNDATION

500 Main Street
Vacaville, CA 95688
(707) 448-6894

Contact: Don Stephenson
Restrictions: Residents of Vacaville, CA, at time of high school graduation; two-year involvement in high school athletics; top 10% of high school graduating class; at least 3.0 GPA in college to maintain aid
$ Given: Average award $900
   Deadline: Early June; interview required

ANNA AND CHARLES STOCKWITZ FUND
FOR EDUCATION OF JEWISH CHILDREN
c/o Wells Fargo Bank
343 Sansome Street, Third Floor
San Francisco, CA 94104

Contact: Teo Schreiber, Director of Loans and Grants program
c/o Stockwitz Fund
1600 Scott Street
San Francisco, CA 94115
(415) 561-1226

Restrictions: Jewish residents of the San Francisco Bay area,
graduates from area high schools; age: 26 or under; financial need
$ Given: 100 grants, up to $5,000

PERRY S. AND STELLA H. TRACY
SCHOLARSHIP FUND
c/o Bank of America
3044 Sacramento Street
Placerville, CA 95667
(916) 622-3634

Contact: Area high schools
Restrictions: Graduates of El Dorado County, CA, high schools or
county residents of at least two years; minimum 3.0. GPA
$ Given: Approximately 125 awards per year; range, $300–$950
    Deadline: April 1, first-time applicants; April 30
    renewal applications

CHARLES A. WINANS MEMORIAL TRUST

Contact: Jack Richardson
Beaumont High School
1591 North Cherry
Beaumont, CA 92223
(909) 845-3171

Restrictions: Beaumont, CA, high school graduates
$ Given: Unavailable

COLORADO

BOETTCHER FOUNDATION SCHOLARSHIPS

Boettcher Foundation
600 17th Street, Suite 2210
South Denver, CO 80202-5422
(303) 534-1938

Contact: Timothy W. Schultz, Executive Director
Restrictions: Colorado residents who are graduating high school seniors; minimum 3.5 GPA; must enroll at a Colorado institution
$ Given: Approximately 40 awards; $ amount unavailable
Deadline: February 1

COLORADO STATE UNIVERSITY

108 Student Services Building
Fort Collins, CO 80523
(970) 491-6321

Contact: Financial Aid Office
Restrictions: Colorado resident; freshmen and transfer students; first-generation college student; financial need
$ Given: Not available

COLORADO UNDERGRADUATE MERIT AWARD

1300 Broadway, 2nd Floor
Denver, CO 80203
(303) 866-2723

Contact: John Ceru, Administrator
Restrictions: Determined by individual schools
$ Given: 9,000 awards, range, $1,000–$2,000

FFA WAL-MART SCHOLARSHIP

P.O. Box 15160
Alexandria, VA 22309-0160
(703) 360-3600

Restrictions: FFA member; freshman-year agriculture major; resident of

Alabama, Arkansas, Arizona, California, Colorado, Connecticut, Delaware, Florida, Georgia, Hawaii, Idaho, Illinois, Indiana, Iowa, Kansas, Kentucky, Louisiana, Maine, Maryland, Michigan, Minnesota, Mississippi, Missouri, Montana, Nebraska, Nevada, New Hampshire, New Mexico, New York, North Carolina, North Dakota, Ohio, Oklahoma, Oregon, Pennsylvania, Puerto Rico, Rhode Island, South Carolina, South Dakota, Tennessee, Texas, Utah, Virginia, Washington State, West Virginia, Wisconsin, or Wyoming
$ Given: Approximately 50 awards of $1,000
  Deadline: February 15

MESA STATE COLLEGE
Robert C. Byrd Honors Scholarship
P.O. Box 2647
Grand Junction, CO 81502
(970) 248-1396

Contact: Financial Aid Department
Restrictions: Freshmen, Colorado residents; minimum 3.8 GPA; minimum 31 ACT or combined SAT score of 1350
$ Given: Not available

SACHS FOUNDATION
90 South Cascade Avenue
Suite 1410
Colorado Springs, CO 80903
(719) 633-2353

Contact: Lisa Harris
Restrictions: Black undergraduate and graduate students who are residents of Colorado; U.S. citizens; enrolled in a two-year or four-year institution; high school students; age: 20 or under
$ Given: 50 grants average $3,000–$4,000
  Deadline: February 15

THE COLORADO MASONS BENEVOLENT
FUND ASSOCIATION
1130 Panorama Drive
Colorado Springs, CO 80904
(303) 290-8544

Contact: Scholarship Administrator
Restrictions: Colorado high school graduates attending Colorado colleges and universities; residents of Colorado; applications available in Colorado public high schools; age: 20 or under; single
$ Given: 10 to 14 grants, up to $20,000
   Deadline: March 15

UNIVERSITY OF COLORADO/BOULDER

Minnie M. Cunningham Scholarship
Campus Box 106
Boulder, CO 80309-0106
(303) 492-5091

Restrictions: Female, Colorado native, current resident; financial need; enrolled in the College of Arts and Sciences
$ Given: Not available

CONNECTICUT

AID FOR PUBLIC COLLEGE STUDENTS GRANTS PROGRAM

Connecticut Department of Higher Education
61 Woodland Street
Hartford, CT 06105

Contact: Financial Aid Office
Restrictions: Students at public Connecticut colleges and universities who are state residents and enrolled at least half-time; financial need
$ Given: Unavailable

LEONARD H. BUCKELEY
SCHOLARSHIP FUND

P.O. Box 1426
New London, CT 06320
(203) 447-1461

Contact: Mrs. Buths
Restrictions: Residents of New London, CT; under 25 years old, undergraduates attending four-year institutions

$ Given: 89 grants; range, $500–$1,000
   Deadline: April 1

CONNECTICUT INDEPENDENT COLLEGE STUDENT GRANT PROGRAM

Connecticut Department of Higher Education
61 Woodland Street
Hartford, CT 06105

Contact: Financial Aid Office
Restrictions: Connecticut residents attending a private Connecticut college or university on at least a half-time basis; financial need
$ Given: Awards up to $7,000

FFA WAL-MART SCHOLARSHIP

P.O. Box 15160
Alexandria, VA 22309-0160
(703) 360-3600

Restrictions: FFA member; freshman-year agriculture major; resident of Alabama, Arkansas, Arizona, California, Colorado, Connecticut, Delaware, Florida, Georgia, Hawaii, Idaho, Illinois, Indiana, Iowa, Kansas, Kentucky, Louisiana, Maine, Maryland, Michigan, Minnesota, Mississippi, Missouri, Montana, Nebraska, Nevada, New Hampshire, New Mexico, New York, North Carolina, North Dakota, Ohio, Oklahoma, Oregon, Pennsylvania, Puerto Rico, Rhode Island, South Carolina, South Dakota, Tennessee, Texas, Utah, Virginia, Washington State, West Virginia, Wisconsin, or Wyoming
$ Given: Approximately 50 awards of $1,000
   Deadline: February 15

FRANK ROSWELL FULLER SCHOLARSHIP

300 Summit Street
Hartford, CT 06106
(860) 297-2046

Restrictions: High school seniors at Hartford County, CT, schools who are members of the Congregational Church; financial need
$ Given: 12 grants annually; range, $1,500–$5,000
   Deadline: April 15

THE MERIDEN FOUNDATION
Webster Trust
P.O. Box 951
Meriden, CT 06450-0951
(203) 235-4456

Contact: Jeffrey F. Otis, Secretary, Distribution Committee
Restrictions: High school seniors who are residents of
Meriden-Wallingford, CT, area
$ Given: Unavailable

JAMES Z. NAURISON SCHOLARSHIP FUND
c/o Fleet Bank
P.O. Box 9006
Springfield, MA 01102-9006
(413) 787-8745

Restrictions: Students from Hampden, Hampshire, Franklin, and Berkshire counties, MA; and Enfield and Suffield counties, CT
$ Given: 450 grants totaling $277,800
   Deadline: April 15

NEW YORK COUNCIL NAVY LEAGUE SCHOLARSHIP
375 Park Avenue
Suite 3408
New York, NY 10152
(212) 355-4960

Contact: Donald Sternberg
Restrictions: Must be dependent of an active or reserve Navy, Marine
Corps, or Coast Guard service member; must be Connecticut, New Jersey,
or New York resident
$ Given: Approximately five $2,500 awards
   Deadline: June 15

SCHOLASTIC ACHIEVEMENT GRANT PROGRAM
Connecticut Department of Higher Education
61 Woodland Street
Hartford, CT 06105

Contact: Financial Aid Office

Restrictions: Connecticut residents attending a school in Connecticut or in a state with reciprocity (Massachusetts, Rhode Island, Vermont, New Hampshire, Maine, Pennsylvania, Delaware, or Washington, DC); students must be in top 20% of class or score 1200 or higher on SAT and have financial need.
$ Given: Awards range, $300–$5,000
    Deadline: February 15

TUITION AID FOR NEEDY STUDENTS PROGRAM
Connecticut Department of Higher Education
61 Woodland Street
Hartford, CT 06105
Restrictions: Connecticut residents who are enrolled at Connecticut state supported schools; financial need
$ Given: Award amounts vary

DELAWARE

ROBERT C. BYRD HONORS SCHOLARSHIP
Delaware Higher Education Commission
820 North French Street
Wilmington, DE 19801
(302) 577-3240

Restrictions: High school student age 20 or under; Delaware resident
$ Given: Grant range, $1,000–$1,500
    Deadline: March 31

DELAWARE HIGHER EDUCATION COMMISSION
820 North French Street, 4th Floor
Wilmington, DE 19801
(302) 577-3240   Fax (302) 577-6765

Restrictions: Residents of Delaware; full-time students with financial needs
$ Given: 16 to 65 awards of $1,000–$1,500
    Deadline: March 31

FFA WAL-MART
SCHOLARSHIP

P.O. Box 15160
Alexandria, VA 22309-0160
(703) 360-3600

Restrictions: FFA member; freshman-year agriculture major; resident of Alabama, Arkansas, Arizona, California, Colorado, Connecticut, Delaware, Florida, Georgia, Hawaii, Idaho, Illinois, Indiana, Iowa, Kansas, Kentucky, Louisiana, Maine, Maryland, Michigan, Minnesota, Mississippi, Missouri, Montana, Nebraska, Nevada, New Hampshire, New Mexico, New York, North Carolina, North Dakota, Ohio, Oklahoma, Oregon, Pennsylvania, Puerto Rico, Rhode Island, South Carolina, South Dakota, Tennessee, Texas, Utah, Virginia, Washington State, West Virginia, Wisconsin, or Wyoming
$ Given: Approximately 50 awards of $1,000
  Deadline: February 15

SCHOLARSHIP
INCENTIVE PROGRAM

Delaware Higher Education Commission
Wilmington, DE 19801

Contact: Nancy Holm, Associate Director
Restrictions: Delaware residents; financial need
$ Given: Renewable awards up to $1,000
  Deadline: April 15

SICO FOUNDATION

P.O. Box 302
15 Mount Joy Street
Mount Joy, PA 17552
(717) 653-1411

Contact: Dawn Zellers, Administrative clerk
Restrictions: Delaware, and some Pennsylvania and Maryland, and New Jersey residents, who attend designated schools; grants only to entering freshmen
$ Given: 120 grants
  Deadline: February 15

DISTRICT OF COLUMBIA

DISTRICT OF COLUMBIA
State Student Incentive Grant
District of Columbia Office of Postsecondary Education,
Research and Assistance
2100 Martin Luther King Avenue SE
Suite 401
Washington, DC 20020
(202) 727-3685

Contact: Jean T. Green
Restrictions: DC residents of at least 15 months prior to application; financial need
$ Given: 1,100 awards; range, $400–$1,000
   Deadline: June 27

WASHINGTON POST
Thomas Ewing Memorial Carrier Scholarship
1150 15th Street, NW
Washington, DC 20079
(202) 334-6060

Contact: Jay O'Hare or Terry Lyn Johnson,
Sales Development Managers
Restrictions: Open to all who are currently carriers of
The Washington Post
$ Given: 35 awards of $1,000–$2,000 per year
   Deadline: January 29

FLORIDA

ROBERT C. BYRD HONORS SCHOLARSHIP
Florida Department of Education
1344 Florida Education Center
Tallhassee, FL 32399

Contact: Joseph Simma
Restrictions: Florida resident attending a Florida school; minimum 3.85 GPA
$ Given: 200 awards of $1,500
   Deadline: April 15

FFA WAL-MART SCHOLARSHIP

P.O. Box 15160
Alexandria, VA 22309-0160
(703) 360-3600

Restrictions: FFA member; freshman-year agriculture major; resident of Alabama, Arkansas, Arizona, California, Colorado, Connecticut, Delaware, Florida, Georgia, Hawaii, Idaho, Illinois, Indiana, Iowa, Kansas, Kentucky, Louisiana, Maine, Maryland, Michigan, Minnesota, Mississippi, Missouri, Montana, Nebraska, Nevada, New Hampshire, New Mexico, New York, North Carolina, North Dakota, Ohio, Oklahoma, Oregon, Pennsylvania, Puerto Rico, Rhode Island, South Carolina, South Dakota, Tennessee, Texas, Utah, Virginia, Washington State, West Virginia, Wisconsin, or Wyoming
$ Given: Approximately 50 awards of $1,000
   Deadline: February 15

FLORIDA DEPARTMENT OF EDUCATION

Office of Student Financial Assistance
Florida Seminole-Miccosukee Indian Scholarship Program
325 West Gaines Street
Room 1344
Florida Education Center
Tallahassee, FL 32399-0400
(904) 488-4095

Restrictions: Florida members of Seminole or Miccosukee Indian tribes; financial need
$ Given: Amount and renewal are decided by each tribe
   Deadline: September 1

FLORIDA DEPARTMENT OF EDUCATION

Office of Student Financial Assistance
Scholarship for Children of Deceased or Disabled Veterans
325 W. Gaines Street

Room 1344
Florida Education Center
Tallahassee, FL 32399-0400

Restrictions: Resident of Florida for minimum five years who is between the ages of 16–22 and enrolled in Florida public institution; parent must be deceased or disabled veteran, or official POW or MIA; undergraduate student
$ Given: Tuition and fees; for two semesters to eight semesters as renewal
   Deadline: April 1

FLORIDA LEADER MAGAZINE

P.O. Box 14081
Gainesville, FL 32604-4081
(352) 373-6907

Restrictions: Florida sophomores, juniors, or seniors enrolled at least half-time; minimum 3.2 GPA
$ Given: Grant range, $500–$1,500
   Deadline: February 1

FLORIDA POSTSECONDARY STUDENT ASSISTANCE GRANT

Florida Department of Education
1344 Florida Education Center
Tallahassee, FL 32399

Contact: Office of Student Financial Assistance
Restrictions: Florida residents attending Florida schools; financial need
$ Given: Not available

FLORIDA PRIVATE STUDENT ASSISTANCE GRANT

Florida Department of Education
1344 Florida Education Center
Tallahassee, FL 32399

Contact: Office of Student Financial Assistance
Restrictions: Florida residents attending private schools; financial need
$ Given: Grant range, $200–$1,500

JOSE MARTI SCHOLARSHIP

Florida Department of Education
1344 Florida Education Center
Tallahassee, FL 32399

Contact: Office of Student Financial Assistance
Restrictions: Hispanic American students who were born in or whose parents were born in an Hispanic country; minimum one-year Florida residency; 3.0 GPA; financial need

GEORGIA

ROBERT C. BYRD HONORS SCHOLARSHIP

Georgia Student Finance Commission
2082 East Exchange Place, Suite 100
Tucker, GA 30084

Contact: Grants Director
Restrictions: High school students age 20 or under who are Georgia residents and maintain at least 3.5 GPA
$ Given: 350 awards of $1,500
    Deadline: April 1

FULLER E. CALLAWAY FOUNDATION

209 Broome Street
La Grange, GA 30240
(706) 884-7348

Contact: J. T. Gresham, General Manager
Restrictions: Resident of Troup County, GA
$ Given: 10 awards of $3,600 (max.) per year, total of $14,400 for four years
    Deadline: February 15

CAPE FOUNDATION, INC.

550 Pharr Road NE, Suite 350
Atlanta, GA 30305
(404) 231-3865

Contact: S. G. Armstrong, Trustee
Restrictions: Foreign students attending Atlanta area institutions
$ Given: Five to 10 awards annually

TY COBB EDUCATIONAL FOUNDATION
Trust Company Bank
P.O. Box 725
Forest Park, GA 30051
(404) 588-8449

Contact: Rosie Atkins, Secretary
Restrictions: Georgia residents who have completed one year in an institute of higher learning; financial need
$ Given: 100 grants; range, $2,000–$3,000
   Deadline: June 15

FFA WAL-MART SCHOLARSHIP
P.O. Box 15160
Alexandria, VA 22309-0160
(703) 360-3600

Restrictions: FFA member; freshman year agriculture major; resident of Alabama, Arkansas, Arizona, California, Colorado, Connecticut, Delaware, Florida, Georgia, Hawaii, Idaho, Illinois, Indiana, Iowa, Kansas, Kentucky, Louisiana, Maine, Maryland, Michigan, Minnesota, Mississippi, Missouri, Montana, Nebraska, Nevada, New Hampshire, New Mexico, New York, North Carolina, North Dakota, Ohio, Oklahoma, Oregon, Pennsylvania, Puerto Rico, Rhode Island, South Carolina, South Dakota, Tennessee, Texas, Utah, Virginia, Washington State, West Virginia, Wisconsin, or Wyoming
$ Given: Approximately 50 awards of $1,000
   Deadline: February 15

GEORGIA STUDENT FINANCE AUTHORITY
Georgia Law Enforcement Personnel Dependents Grant
2082 East Exchange Place, Suite 100
Tucker, GA 30084
(404) 493-5444

Contact: Grants Director

Restrictions: U.S. citizens, enrolled in a Georgia postsecondary school; residents of Georgia; children of Georgia law enforcement officers, firemen, or prison guards killed or disabled in the line of duty; must stay in Georgia while receiving funds; demonstrate financial need
$ Given: Unspecified number of $2,000 grants, renewable to maximum of $8,000 over a four-year period
Deadline: August 1, or 30 days prior to beginning of academic term

GEORGIA STUDENT FINANCE AUTHORITY
Georgia Student Incentive Grant
2082 East Exchange Place, Suite 100
Tucker, GA 30084
(404) 493-5453

Contact: Grants Director
Restrictions: U.S. citizens, resident of Georgia (12 months prior to registration) in full-time Georgia institution; financial need
$ Given: Unspecified number of $300–$5,000 grants per year renewable (not given during summer terms)
Deadline: June 1

GEORGIA TUITION EQUALIZATION GRANT
Georgia Student Finance Commission
2082 East Exchange Place, Suite 100
Tucker, GA 30084

Contact: Grants Director
Restrictions: Georgia residents attending Georgia schools
$ Given: $1,000 awards per year

HOPE GRANT PROGRAM
Georgia Student Finance Commission
2082 East Exchange Place
Suite 100
Tucker, GA 30084

Contact: Grants Director
Restrictions: Tuition and fees not covered by federal aid for Georgia residents attending Georgia institutions; must maintain minimum 3.0 GPA
$ Given: $1,500 awards per year; renewable

THE DANIEL ASHLEY & IRENE HOUSTON JEWELL MEMORIAL FOUNDATION

c/o American National Bank
P.O. Box 1638
Chattanooga, TN 37401
(615) 757-3203

Restrictions: Dade, Catoosa, and Walker County, GA, residents who are high school seniors
$ Given: 11 grants with an average of $1,500

STUDENT AID FOUNDATION

2520 East Piedmont Road, Suite 180
Marietta, GA 30062
(770) 973-0256 or (770) 973-7077

Contact: Catherine W. Reynolds
Restrictions: Female residents of Georgia and female students at Georgia schools; must be full-time student and maintain at least 3.0 GPA
$ Loaned: 50 loans per year; $2,500 per year for undergraduate; $3,000 for graduate; $3,000 per year for freshmen and sophomores; $4,000 per year for juniors and seniors

HAROLD AND SARA WETHERBEE FOUNDATION

c/o First State Bank and Trust Company
P.O. Box 8
Albany, GA 31703
(912) 432-8090

Contact: Thomas B. Clifton, Jr.
Restrictions: Residents of Dougherty and Lee counties, GA
$ Given: 20 grants; range, $500–$2,000
   Deadline: April 15

HAWAII

FFA WAL-MART SCHOLARSHIP

P.O. Box 15160
Alexandria, VA 22309-0160
(703) 360-3600

Restrictions: FFA member; freshman-year agriculture major; resident of Alabama, Arkansas, Arizona, California, Colorado, Connecticut, Delaware, Florida, Georgia, Hawaii, Idaho, Illinois, Indiana, Iowa, Kansas, Kentucky, Louisiana, Maine, Maryland, Michigan, Minnesota, Mississippi, Missouri, Montana, Nebraska, Nevada, New Hampshire, New Mexico, New York, North Carolina, North Dakota, Ohio, Oklahoma, Oregon, Pennsylvania, Puerto Rico, Rhode Island, South Carolina, South Dakota, Tennessee, Texas, Utah, Virginia, Washington State, West Virginia, Wisconsin, or Wyoming
$ Given: Approximately 50 awards of $1,000
  Deadline: February 15

FUKUNAGA SCHOLARSHIP FOUNDATION
900 Fort Street Mall, Suite 500
Honolulu, HI 96813
(808) 521-6511

Contact: Scholarship Selection Committee
Restrictions: U.S. citizens; Hawaii business students; Hawaii residence; average 3.0 grade point necessary
$ Given: 12 to 15 grants; range, $1,500–$2,000
  Deadline: April 15

BARBARA ALICE MOWER MEMORIAL SCHOLARSHIP
Kilohana United Methodist Church
1536 Kamole Street
Honolulu, HI 96821

Contact: Nancy A. Mower
Restrictions: College juniors or seniors, female; Hawaii residents with a strong interest in women's studies
$ Given: Up to 20 $1,000–$3,000 awards
  Deadline: May 1

PACIFIC PRINTING AND IMAGING ASSOCIATION
Educational Trust Scholarships
180 Nickerson, Suite 102
Seattle, WA 98109

Contact: Jim Olsen
Restrictions: Students studying printing, print management, or graphic

arts technology. Must live in Washington, Oregon, Arkansas, Idaho, Montana, or Hawaii.

$ Given: 12 awards, range, $500–$2,500; renewable
    Deadline: April 1

IDAHO

FFA WAL-MART SCHOLARSHIP
P.O. Box 15160
Alexandria, VA 22309-0160
(703) 360-3600

Restrictions: FFA member; freshman-year agriculture major; resident of Alabama, Arkansas, Arizona, California, Colorado, Connecticut, Delaware, Florida, Georgia, Hawaii, Idaho, Illinois, Indiana, Iowa, Kansas, Kentucky, Louisiana, Maine, Maryland, Michigan, Minnesota, Mississippi, Missouri, Montana, Nebraska, Nevada, New Hampshire, New Mexico, New York, North Carolina, North Dakota, Ohio, Oklahoma, Oregon, Pennsylvania, Puerto Rico, Rhode Island, South Carolina, South Dakota, Tennessee, Texas, Utah, Virginia, Washington State, West Virginia, Wisconsin, or Wyoming

$ Given: Approximately 50 awards of $1,000
    Deadline: February 15

PAUL L. FOWLER MEMORIAL SCHOLARSHIP
State Board of Education
Room 307 Len B. Jordan Building
P.O. Box 83720
Boise, ID 83720-0037
(208) 334-2270

Contact: High School Guidance office or Scholarship Assistant
Restrictions: Idaho residents in an institution of higher learning, enrolled as full-time students; based on class rank, ACT scores.
$ Given: Two grants for $2,830 each
    Deadline: January 31

PACIFIC PRINTING
AND IMAGING ASSOCIATION
Educational Trust Scholarships
180 Nickerson, Suite 102
Seattle, WA 98109

Contact: Jim Olsen
Restrictions: Students studying printing, print management, or graphic arts technology. Must live in Washington, Oregon, Arkansas, Idaho, Montana, or Hawaii.
$ Given: 12 awards, range, $500–$2,500; renewable
　Deadline: April 1

POTLATCH FOUNDATION
FOR HIGHER EDUCATION
P.O. Box 193591
San Francisco, CA 94119-3591
(415) 576-8829

Contact: Jenni Rogers
Restrictions: Residents of Arizona, California, Idaho, Nevada, and Minnesota (within 30 miles of a Potlatch Corporation facility); financial need; academic achievement
$ Given: 80 grants
　Deadlines: February 15 for new applications and July 1 for scholarship renewals

STATE OF IDAHO SCHOLARSHIP
State Board of Education
P.O. Box 83720
Boise, ID 83720-0037
(208) 334-2270

Contact: High School Guidance Office or Scholarship assistance
Restrictions: Graduates of Idaho high schools to attend full-time Idaho institutions
$ Given: 25 grants of $2,650; renewable for four years
　Deadline: January 31

TREACY COMPANY
Scholarship for Freshmen or Sophomore Students
Box 1700
Helena, MT 59624-1700
(406) 442-3632

Contact: James O'Connell
Restrictions: Residents of or students attending institutions in Idaho, Montana, North Dakota, and South Dakota
$ Given: 25 to 35 grants; average grant, $400
   Deadline: June 15

ILLINOIS

JOSEPH BLAZEK
FOUNDATION
8 South Michigan Avenue
Suite 801
Chicago, IL 60603
(312) 236-3882

Contact: Samuel S. Brown, Executive Director
Restrictions: Cook County, IL, high school senior students planning to major in engineering, math, chemistry, physics, or related scientific fields.
$ Given: $1,000 per year for four years
   Deadline: February 1 of high school senior year

KATHERINE BOGARDUS TRUST
c/o The John Warner Bank
P.O. Box 679
Clinton, IL 61727
(217) 935-3144

Contact: Kathy McNees, Trust Officer
Restrictions: High school graduates in De Witt County, IL; descendants of first cousins of trust's founder
$ Loaned: Award amounts vary

HENRY BUNN MEMORIAL FUND

Bank One
P.O. Box 19266
Springfield, IL 62794-9266
(217) 525-9600

Restrictions: Graduating high school seniors who are residents of Sangamon County, IL
$ Given: Grant range, $500–$1,000
   Deadline: March 1

THE WILLIAM, AGNES & ELIZABETH BURGESS MEMORIAL SCHOLARSHIP FUND

c/o Mid-Illinois Bank and Trust
P.O. Box 499
Mattoon, IL 61938
(217) 234-7454

Contact: Senior Trust Officer
Restrictions: Mattoon Community School District high school graduates
$ Given: Seven grants; average $800 per year
   Deadline: April 15

SUSAN COOK HOUSE EDUCATIONAL TRUST

Bank One
P.O. Box 19266
Springfield, IL 62794-9266
(217) 525-9600

Restrictions: Grants to high school seniors who are residents of Singamon County, IL
$ Given: Grant range, $500–$1,000
   Deadline: March 1

FFA WAL-MART SCHOLARSHIP

P.O. Box 15160
Alexandria, VA 22309-0160
(703) 360-3600

Restrictions: FFA member; freshman-year agriculture major; resident of

Alabama, Arkansas, Arizona, California, Colorado, Connecticut, Delaware, Florida, Georgia, Hawaii, Idaho, Illinois, Indiana, Iowa, Kansas, Kentucky, Louisiana, Maine, Maryland, Michigan, Minnesota, Mississippi, Missouri, Montana, Nebraska, Nevada, New Hampshire, New Mexico, New York, North Carolina, North Dakota, Ohio, Oklahoma, Oregon, Pennsylvania, Puerto Rico, Rhode Island, South Carolina, South Dakota, Tennessee, Texas, Utah, Virginia, Washington State, West Virginia, Wisconsin, or Wyoming
$ Given: Approximately 50 awards of $1,000
   Deadline: February 15

BOYNTON GILLESPIE MEMORIAL FUND
Heritage Federal Building
Sparta, IL 62286
(618) 443-4430

Contact: John Clendenin, Trustee
Restrictions: Sparta, IL, area residents
$ Given: 104 grants totaling $76,475; range, $475–$500
   Deadline: May 1

ILLINOIS DEPARTMENT OF THE AMERICAN LEGION SCHOLARSHIPS
P.O. Box 2910
Bloomington, IL 61702-2910
(309) 663-0361

Contact: Department Adjutant
Restrictions: Dependent children of members of Illinois American Legion who are high school seniors
$ Given: 20 grants of $1,000
   Deadline: March 15

ILLINOIS DEPARTMENT OF THE AMERICAN LEGION SCOUTING SCHOLARSHIPS
P.O. Box 2910
Bloomington, IL 61702-2910
(309) 663-0361

Contact: Legion Scout Chairman
Restrictions: Qualified senior Boy Scouts who are residents of Illinois;

must submit 500 word essay on Legion's "Americanism" and scouting program; must be senior scouts or explorers
$ Given: One $1,000 scholarship and four runner-up scholarships of $200 each
> **Deadline:**   April 30

ILLINOIS EDUCATIONAL OPPORTUNITIES FOR CHILDREN OF VETERANS

Illinois Department of Veteran Affairs
P.O. Box 19432
Springfield, IL 62794-9432

Contact: Eva Palmer
Restrictions: Illinois residents who are children of veterans who died or became totally disabled during World War II, the Korean War, or Vietnam War
$ Given: Not available

ILLINOIS STUDENT ASSISTANCE COMMISSION

Benefits for Survivors of Policemen and Firemen
1755 Lake Cook Road
Deerfield, IL 60015-5209
(217) 782-6767; (800) 899-4722

Restrictions: Residents of Illinois; children, 25 and under, or dependent wife of police and firemen killed in the line of duty; for study at Illinois institutions
$ Given: All entitled receive up to $3,800

ILLINOIS STUDENT ASSISTANCE COMMISSION

Merit Recognition Scholarship
1755 Lake Cook Road
Deerfield, IL 60015-5209
(708) 948-8550

Contact: Manager, Scholarships and Grants
Restrictions: Illinois residents ranked in top 5% of high school graduating class who plan to attend approved Illinois postsecondary institutions at least half-time
$ Given: Average award $1,000

ILLINOIS STUDENT ASSISTANCE COMMISSION
Monetary Award Program
1755 Lake Cook Road
Deerfield, IL 60015-5209
(708) 948-8550; (800) 899-4722

Restrictions: Residents of Illinois; new or continuing students with financial need
$ Given: Approximately 100,000 grants $400–$4,000, renewable for five years
Deadlines: Renewals: May 31; new applicants: September 30

ILLINOIS STUDENT ASSISTANCE COMMISSION
Scholarships for Survivors or Dependents of Correctional Workers
1755 Lake Cook Road
Deerfield, IL 60015-5209
(800) 899-4722

Restrictions: Residents of Illinois; dependents of employees of Illinois Department of Corrections killed or 90% disabled in the line of duty after January 1, 1960; U.S. citizens
$ Given: All entitled receive up to $3,800, for eight semesters

MARCUS & THERESA LEVIE EDUCATIONAL FUND
c/o Jewish Federation of Metropolitan Chicago
1 South Franklin Street
Chicago, IL 60606
(312) 357-4521

Contact: Lea Gruhn
Restrictions: Jewish residents of Cook County, IL, for at least one year before attending college; financial need
$ Given: 32 grants totaling $137,000; average, $5,000
Deadline: March 1

MCFARLAND CHARITABLE FOUNDATION
c/o Havana National Bank Trustee
P.O. Box 200
112 South Orange Street
Havana, IL 62644-0200

Contact: Linda Butler, Vice President and Senior Trust Officer
Restrictions: Nursing students from Macon County, IL; financial need
$ Given: Three to five grants from $1,000–$15,000
  Deadline: May 1

ELLA G. MCKEE FOUNDATION

c/o First National Bank
P.O. Box 40
Vandalia, IL 62471
(618) 283-1141

Contact: Liz Heinzmann
Restrictions: Residents of Fayette County, IL (minimum four-year residency)
$ Given: 63 grants totaling $64,028; range, $900–$1,800
  Deadline: June 1

EDWIN T. MEREDITH FOUNDATION

Contact: Local County 4-H Office or State 4-H Office
Restrictions: Must be a 4-H member for at least one year; outstanding achievement; resident of Illinois, Indiana, Iowa, Kansas, Michigan, Minnesota, Missouri, Nebraska, New York, North Dakota, Ohio, Oklahoma, Pennsylvania, South Dakota, or Wisconsin
$ Given: Approximately three awards of $1,000
  Deadline: September 1

MINORITY TEACHERS
OF ILLINOIS SCHOLARSHIP

Illinois Student Assistance Commission
1755 Lake Cook Road
Deerfield, IL 60015-5209

Contact: Manager, Scholarships and Grants
Restrictions: Minority students who plan to become teachers at the elementary or secondary school level; must attend Illinois school, be sophomore or higher, and sign teaching commitment to teach one year for each year assistance is received.
$ Given: Up to $5,000 per year
  Deadline: August 1

REBEKAH SCHOLARSHIP AWARD
Grand Lodge of Illinois
P.O. Box 248
Lincoln, IL 62656

Contact: Scholarship Committee
Restrictions: Scholarship for use in freshman year; under 20; resident of Illinois; minimum 2.5 GPA
$ Given: 15–18 awards, range, $500–$1,000
  Deadline: March 1

JACOB STUMP JR. & CLARA STUMP
MEMORIAL SCHOLARSHIP FUND
c/o Central National Bank of Mattoon
1632 Broadway Avenue, Suite 300
Mattoon, IL 61938
(217) 234-6430

Contact: Trust Officer
Restrictions: High school graduates from Coles, Cumberland, Douglas, and Moultrie counties who will attend state-supported Illinois colleges
$ Given: 82 grants totaling $82,000; grants per year averaging $1,000 for four years
  Deadline: April 15

THE SWISS BENEVOLENT
SOCIETY OF CHICAGO
6440 North Bosworth Avenue
Chicago, IL 60626

Contact: Prof. E. Schmocker, Scholarship Chairman
Restrictions: Persons of Swiss descent resident in Illinois, Wisconsin; for college students, 3.5 GPA; for high school students, 26 on American college test or 1050 on SAT
$ Given: 30 awards; average, $750–$2,500
  Deadline: March 1

INDIANA

THOMAS L., MYRTLE R., ARCH
AND EVA ALEXANDER SCHOLARSHIP FUND
Citizens National Bank
P.O. Box 719
Evansville, IN 47705
(812) 464-3217

Contact: High School Guidance Counselor
Restrictions: Graduating students of Posey County, IN, high schools only, based on academic achievement
$ Given: 10 scholarships per year, 9 scholastic and 1 music; first year, $2,000; second year, range, $560–$7,500
  Deadline: Varies by high school

FRED A. BRYAN
COLLEGIATE STUDENTS FUND
Norwest Bank, Trust Dept.
112 West Jefferson Boulevard
South Bend, IN 46601
(219) 237-3342

Contact: Pamela Henderson
Restrictions: Male graduates of South Bend high school; preference given to Boy Scouts in good standing for two years prior to application; must be South Bend resident
$ Given: Six grants of approximately $1,500 each, renewable for four years
  Deadline: March 1

GEORGE W. BURKETT TRUST
c/o First National Bank of Monterey
6 East Main Street
Monterey, IN 46960

Special Contact:
Coleen McCarthy, Scholarship Administrator
(219) 896-2158

Contact:
Know Community High School
Allan Bourf
 # 2 Redskin Trail
Knox, IN 36534
(219) 772-3712

North Judson-San Pierre Schools
Roger Sutton
960 Campell Dr.
North Judson, IN 46366
(219) 896-2155

Oregon-Davis High School
William Renstschler
P.O. Box 65
Hamlet, IN 46532
(219) 867-2111

ROBERT C. BYRD HONORS SCHOLARSHIP
Indiana State Student Assistance Commission
150 West Market Street, Suite 500
Indianapolis, IN 46204

Contact: Special Programs Director
Restrictions: Indiana resident attending Indiana school; must score at least 1300 on SAT or 31 on ACT
$ Given: 428 awards of $1,500
  Deadline: April 22

OLIVE B. COLE FOUNDATION, INC.
6207 Constitution Drive
Fort Wayne, IN 46804
(219) 436-2182

Contact: Mrs. Glenn Tipton
Restrictions: High school graduates, residents of Noble County, IN, area
$ Given: Average grant, $900
  Deadline: March 31

CULVER COMMUNITY HIGH SCHOOL

William F. Mills
222 North Ohio Street
Culver, IN 46511
(219) 842-3364

Restrictions: Students graduating from the high schools listed on page 40
$ Given: Average grant, $500
 Deadline: April 15

EISENHOWER MEMORIAL SCHOLARSHIP FOUNDATION

303 North Curry Pike
P.O. Box 223
Bloomington, IN 47408-2502
(812) 332-2257

Contact: E. M. Sears, Executive Director
Restrictions: Age 20 or under; enrolled at a four-year institution in Indiana; single; interest in leadership; 2.5 GPA; U.S. citizens
$ Given: 30 to 35 grants; range, $2,500–$10,000

FFA WAL-MART SCHOLARSHIP

P.O. Box 15160
Alexandria, VA 22309-0160
(703) 360-3600

Restrictions: FFA member; freshman-year agriculture major; resident of Alabama, Arkansas, Arizona, California, Colorado, Connecticut, Delaware, Florida, Georgia, Hawaii, Idaho, Illinois, Indiana, Iowa, Kansas, Kentucky, Louisiana, Maine, Maryland, Michigan, Minnesota, Mississippi, Missouri, Montana, Nebraska, Nevada, New Hampshire, New Mexico, New York, North Carolina, North Dakota, Ohio, Oklahoma, Oregon, Pennsylvania, Puerto Rico, Rhode Island, South Carolina, South Dakota, Tennessee, Texas, Utah, Virginia, Washington State, West Virginia, Wisconsin, or Wyoming
$ Given: Approximately 50 awards of $1,000
 Deadline: February 15

INDIANA NURSING SCHOLARSHIP FUND

Indiana State Student Assistance Commission
150 West Market Street, Suite 500
Indianapolis, IN 46204-2811

Contact: Special Programs Director
Restrictions: Indiana residents pursuing nursing degrees at Indiana schools; minimum 2.5 GPA; financial need. Grant recipients must agree to work as a nurse for at least two years after graduation.
$ Given: Awards up to $5,000

EDWIN T. MEREDITH FOUNDATION

Contact: Local County 4-H Office or State 4-H Office
Restrictions: Must be 4-H member for at least one year; outstanding achievement; resident of Illinois, Indiana, Iowa, Kansas, Michigan, Minnesota, Missouri, Nebraska, New York, North Dakota, Ohio, Oklahoma, Pennsylvania, South Dakota, or Wisconsin
$ Given: Approximately three awards of $1,000
   Deadline: September 1

RUTH M. MINEAR
EDUCATIONAL TRUST
c/o Norwest Bank, Wabash, N.A.
P.O. Box 397
841 North Cass
Wabash, IN 46992
(219) 563-1116

Contact: Trust Officer
Restrictions: Graduates of Wabash High School
$ Given: Range, $500–$2,000
   Deadline: Mid-February

MINORITY TEACHER AND SPECIAL
EDUCATION SERVICES SCHOLARSHIP
Indiana State Student Assistance Commission
150 West Market Street, Suite 500
Indianapolis, IN 46204-2811

Contact: Program Director
Restrictions: African-American or Hispanic Indiana residents, minimum 2.0 GPA, seeking teacher certification in special education or physical occupational therapy. Upon certification, recipients are required to teach in Indiana.
$ Given: $1,000 per year; renewable

NICCUM EDUCATIONAL
TRUST FOUNDATION

c/o NDB Bank
P.O. Box 27
Goshen, IN 46527-0027
(219) 533-2175

Contact: Rod Diller or JoAnne Pickens
Restrictions: Graduates of public schools in Goshen, Elkort, St. Joseph, La Grange, Noble, Marshall, IN, area
$ Given: Grants totaling $4,800; range, $800–$1,500
  Deadline: March 1

NUCOR FOUNDATION, INC.

2100 Rexford Road
Charlotte, NC 28211
(704) 366-7000

Contact: Elizabeth Wells
Restrictions: Children of Nucor, Inc., employees only; must maintain 2.0 GPA
$ Given: Average $2,200 per year for four years
  Deadline: March 1

STATE STUDENT ASSISTANCE COMMISSION
OF INDIANA HIGHER EDUCATION AWARDS

150 West Market Street, Suite 500
Indianapolis, IN 46204-2811
(317) 232-2350

Restrictions: Indiana residents for study full time at an eligible Indiana institution; financial need; preference to students pursuing religious study
$ Given: 3,200 grants of $1,200–$2,700
  Deadline: March 1

STATE STUDENT ASSISTANCE
COMMISSION OF INDIANA

Hoosier Scholarships
150 West Market Street, Suite 500
Indianapolis, IN 46204-2811
(317) 232-2350

Restrictions: Seniors of Indiana high schools for study at an eligible Indiana institution; must be in top 20% of class
$ Given: 800 grants of $500; nonrenewable
   Deadline: March 1

TWENTY-FIRST CENTURY
SCHOLARS AWARD

Office of Twenty-First Scholars
150 West Market Street
Suite 500
Indianapolis, IN 46204-2811

Contact: Philip A. Seabrook, Director
Restrictions: Indiana residents attending Indiana schools; financial need
$ Given: $1,000–$3,000 awards; renewable

IOWA

AMERICAN LEGION
AUXILIARY DEPARTMENT OF IOWA

Children of Veterans Scholarship
720 Lyon Street
Des Moines, IA 50309

Contact: Marlene M. Valentine, Secretary-Treasurer
Restrictions: Iowa resident enrolled full time at an Iowa school who is a child of a veteran who served during eligibility dates for membership in the American Legion; freshman year only
$ Given: Approximately 13 $200 awards
   Deadline: March 1

EASTER SEAL SOCIETY OF IOWA, INC.

James L. and Lovon Mallory Annual Disability Scholarship
P.O. Box 4002
Des Moines, IA 50333
(515) 289-1933

Contact: Deb Wissink

Restrictions: Residents of Iowa who are graduating from high school who have a permanent disability; top 40% of class or have 2.8 GPA; financial need
$ Given: Two grants from $750–$1,000
  Deadline: April 15

FFA WAL-MART SCHOLARSHIP

P.O. Box 15160
Alexandria, VA 22309-0160
(703) 360-3600

Restrictions: FFA member; freshman-year agriculture major; resident of Alabama, Arkansas, Arizona, California, Colorado, Connecticut, Delaware, Florida, Georgia, Hawaii, Idaho, Illinois, Indiana, Iowa, Kansas, Kentucky, Louisiana, Maine, Maryland, Michigan, Minnesota, Mississippi, Missouri, Montana, Nebraska, Nevada, New Hampshire, New Mexico, New York, North Carolina, North Dakota, Ohio, Oklahoma, Oregon, Pennsylvania, Puerto Rico, Rhode Island, South Carolina, South Dakota, Tennessee, Texas, Utah, Virginia, Washington State, West Virginia, Wisconsin, or Wyoming
$ Given: Approximately 50 awards of $1,000
  Deadline: February 15

FAHRNEY EDUCATION FOUNDATION

c/o First Star Bank
123 East Third Street
Ottumwa, IA 52501
(515) 683-1641

Contact: Scholarship Committee
Restrictions: Residents of Wapello County, IA, who are planning to attend a college in Iowa
$ Given: Grants of $1,500
  Deadline: February 15

IOWA COLLEGE STUDENT AID COMMISSION

Iowa Technical Tuition Grant
200 10th Street (Fourth Floor)
Des Moines, IA 50309-3609
(515) 281-3501

Contact: Vickie Adair
Restrictions: Residents of Iowa to attend privately supported eligible colleges, universities, business schools, nursing schools; financial need; full-time attendance
$ Given: Grants up to $3,150 a year
  Deadline: April 30

IOWA COLLEGE STUDENT AID COMMISSION
Iowa Tuition Grant Program
200 10th Street (Fourth Floor)
Des Moines, IA 50309-3609
(515) 281-3501

Contact: Vickie Adair
Restrictions: Iowa public college for a vocational-technical career education or career option program; financial need; full-time
$ Given: Grants up to $600 a year; One renewable
  Deadline: April 20

IOWA COLLEGE STUDENT AID COMMISSION
State of Iowa Scholar and Monetary Scholarships
200 10th Street (Fourth Floor)
Des Moines, IA 50309-3609
(515) 281-3501

Contact: Vicki Adair
Restrictions: Iowa high school seniors (just freshman year) who plan to attend an eligible Iowa college or university; criteria: top 15% of class, ACT and SAT test score, financial need
$ Given: 1,600 awards of $410 per year
  Deadline: December 1

IOWA GRANTS
Iowa College Student Aid Commission
200 10th Street, Fourth Floor
Des Moines, IA 50309-3609
(515) 281-3501

Restrictions: Iowa resident enrolled at least half-time in an Iowa school
$ Given: Awards up to $1,000

EDWIN T. MEREDITH FOUNDATION

Contact: Local County 4-H Office or State 4-H Office
Restrictions: Must be a 4-H member for at least one year; outstanding achievement; resident of Illinois, Indiana, Iowa, Kansas, Michigan, Minnesota, Missouri, Nebraska, New York, North Dakota, Ohio, Oklahoma, Pennsylvania, South Dakota, or Wisconsin
$ Given: Approximately three awards of $1,000
Deadline: September 1

ORATORIAL CONTEST SCHOLARSHIP

720 Lyon Street
Des Moines, IA 50309

Restrictions: Must attend high school in Iowa, enter contest locally, and attend IA college or university
$ Given: Three awards, range $400–$2,000
Deadline: September

ELMER O. AND IDA PRESTON EDUCATIONAL TRUST

801 Grand Avenue
Suite 3700
Des Moines, IA 50309
(515) 243-4191

Contact: Monica Morgan, Trust Administrative Assistant
Restrictions: Male Protestant students residing in Iowa attending an Iowa college or university
$ Given: Grants and loans totaling $100,000; range, $250–$7,000
Deadline: June 30

PRITCHARD EDUCATIONAL FUND

c/o Cherokee State Bank
212 West Willow Street
Cherokee, IA 51012
(712) 225-3000

Contact: Jim Mohn, Foundation Manager
Restrictions: Students attending Cherokee County schools
$ Loaned: 160 loans totaling $200,000; average, $1,200; renewable yearly
Deadline: July 15

KANSAS

CLAUDE AND INA BREY MEMORIAL ENDOWMENT FUND
c/o The Mercantile Bank of Topeka
P.O. Box 192
Topeka, KS 66601-0192
(913) 291-1000

Contact: Becky Miller
Restrictions: Scholarships only to fourth-degree Kansas Grange members
$ Given: Seven grants of $500 each
Deadline: April 15

JAMES A. AND JULIET L. DAVIS FOUNDATION, INC.
418 First National Center
P.O. Box 2027
Hutchinson, KS 67504-2027
(316) 663-5021

Contact: Mr. Chalfant
Restrictions: Awarded by Hutchinson High School committee for graduates attending college in Kansas or Montana.
$ Given: Three for men, three for women; $10,000 per student

FFA WAL-MART SCHOLARSHIP
P.O. Box 15160
Alexandria, VA 22309-0160
(703) 360-3600

Restrictions: FFA member; freshman-year agriculture major; resident of Alabama, Arkansas, Arizona, California, Colorado, Connecticut, Delaware, Florida, Georgia, Hawaii, Idaho, Illinois, Indiana, Iowa, Kansas, Kentucky, Louisiana, Maine, Maryland, Michigan, Minnesota, Mississippi, Missouri, Montana, Nebraska, Nevada, New Hampshire, New Mexico, New York, North Carolina, North Dakota, Ohio, Oklahoma, Oregon, Pennsylvania, Puerto Rico, Rhode Island, South Carolina, South Dakota, Tennessee, Texas, Utah, Virginia, Washington State, West Virginia, Wisconsin, or Wyoming
$ Given: Approximately 50 awards of $1,000
Deadline: February 15

DANE G. HANSEN FOUNDATION

P.O. Box 187
Logan, KS 67646
(913) 689-4832

Contact: Raymond Lappin, Chairman Scholarship Committee
Restrictions: High school seniors residing in northwest Kansas;
3.5 GPA
$ Given: 6 grants of $3,500
   Deadline: October 1

R. L. AND ELSO HELVERING TRUST

c/o Edward F. Wiegers
P.O. Box 468, 1114 Broadway
Marysville, KS 66508
(913) 562-2375

Restrictions: Marshall County high school seniors planning to attend
Kansas colleges
$ Given: Unavailable

KANSAS BOARD OF REGENTS

Kansas Tuition Grant
700 Southwest Harrison, Suite 1410
Topeka, KS 66603
(913) 296-3517

Contact: Christie Crenshaw, Financial Aid Director
Restrictions: Residents of Kansas enrolled at private schools; full time
study; financial need
$ Given: 3,500 grants of up to $1,700; renewable
   Deadline: April 1. Apply directly to institution

KANSAS BOARD OF REGENTS

Security Benefit Building
State Scholarship
700 Southwest Harrison, Suite 1410
Topeka, KS 66603
(913) 296-3517

Contact: Christie Crenshaw, Financial Aid Director

Restrictions: High school graduate; enrolled at an eligible Kansas institution; satisfactory academic performance; financial need; for students designated as state scholars
$ Given: 1,200 grants from $200; renewable
   Deadline: April 1

KANSAS COMMISSION OF VETERANS' AFFAIRS SCHOLARSHIPS

Jayhawk Tower
700 Southwest Jackson Street, #701
Topeka, KS 66603
(913) 296-3976

Contact: Don Hibler
Restrictions: Children of persons who entered U.S. armed forces as a resident of Kansas and who were killed in action in Vietnam or became POWs or MIAs; no age restriction; Kansas residents
$ Given: Tuition and fees waived by Kansas law
   Deadline: Prior to enrollment

KANSAS MINORITY SCHOLARSHIP PROGRAM

Kansas Board of Regents
700 Southwest Harrison, Suite 1410
Topeka, KS 66603
(913) 296-3517

Restrictions: Minority Kansas residents attending Kansas schools; scholastic ability; financial need
$ Given: Renewable scholarships up to $1,500 per year
   Deadline: April 1

KANSAS NURSING SCHOLARSHIP PROGRAM

Kansas Board of Regents
700 Southwest Harrison, Suite 1410
Topeka, KS 66603
(913) 296-3517

Restrictions: Kansas residents enrolled in nursing program. Recipients are required to work one year for each year of scholarship aid received.
$ Given: $2,500–$3,500 per year
   Deadline: May 1

KANSAS TEACHER SCHOLARSHIP PROGRAM

Kansas Board of Regents
700 Southwest Harrison, Suite 1410
Topeka, KS 66603
(913) 296-3517

Restrictions: Students pursuing teaching careers. Recipients must teach in a "hard to fill" subject in Kansas for one year for each year of monies received.
$ Given: $5,000 per year; renewable
   Deadline: April 1

EDWIN T. MEREDITH FOUNDATION

Contact: Local County 4-H Office or State 4-H Office
Restrictions: Must be a 4-H member for at least one year; outstanding achievement; resident of Illinois, Indiana, Iowa, Kansas, Michigan, Minnesota, Missouri, Nebraska, New York, North Dakota, Ohio, Oklahoma, Pennsylvania, South Dakota, or Wisconsin
$ Given: Approximately three awards of $1,000
   Deadline: September 1

LAURA E. PORTER TRUST

Drawer H
Pratt, KS 67124
(316) 672-5533

Contact: J. W. Van Blaricum, Bill Hampton, Jr., Mike Lewis, Trustees
Restrictions: Male graduates of Pratt County Community College, KS, to further their education at a university approved by the trustees
$ Given: Amounts vary

KENTUCKY

FFA WAL-MART SCHOLARSHIP

P.O. Box 15160
Alexandria, VA 22309-0160
(703) 360-3600

Restrictions: FFA member; freshman-year agriculture major; resident of Alabama, Arkansas, Arizona, California, Colorado, Connecticut, Delaware, Florida, Georgia, Hawaii, Idaho, Illinois, Indiana, Iowa, Kansas, Kentucky, Louisiana, Maine, Maryland, Michigan, Minnesota, Mississippi, Missouri, Montana, Nebraska, Nevada, New Hampshire, New Mexico, New York, North Carolina, North Dakota, Ohio, Oklahoma, Oregon, Pennsylvania, Puerto Rico, Rhode Island, South Carolina, South Dakota, Tennessee, Texas, Utah, Virginia, Washington State, West Virginia, Wisconsin, or Wyoming
$ Given: Approximately 50 awards of $1,000
  Deadline: February 15

BLANCHE AND THOMAS HOPE MEMORIAL FUND
c/o National City Bank
P.O. Box 1270
Ashland, KY 41105-1270
(606) 329-2900

Restrictions: Graduating seniors from Boyd and Greenup counties, KY, and Lawrence County, OH
$ Given: Range, $90–$2,500
  Deadline: March 1

KENTUCKY CENTER FOR VETERANS AFFAIRS BENEFITS FORVETERANS AND THEIR DEPENDENTS
Department of Veterans Affairs
545 South Third Street
Louisville, KY 40202-9095
(502) 588-4447

Contact: Larry W. Garrett, Coordinator
Restrictions: Residents of Kentucky; U.S. armed forces or National Guard veterans, children under 25 or non-remarried spouses of veterans killed, permanently disabled, or listed as POWs or MIAs in recognized hostile actions; undergraduate study; attend a Kentucky state college
$ Given: Tuition waivers

KENTUCKY DEPARTMENT OF EDUCATION
Minority Educator Scholarships
Kentucky Department of Education
Capitol Plaza Tower, 1st Floor
Frankfort, KY 40601-9095

Contact: Minority Scholarship Program
Restrictions: Minority sophomores, juniors or seniors enrolled in a teaching program; Kentucky resident; must teach in the state of Kentucky for one year for each award
$ Given: $3,000

KENTUCKY TUITION GRANT
Kentucky Higher Education Assistance Authority
1050 U.S. 127 South
Frankfort, KY 40601-4323

Restrictions: Kentucky residents enrolled full-time at a private Kentucky college or university; financial need
$ Given: Approximately 6,500 grants of $1,500

THE LOUISVILLE COMMUNITY FOUNDATION, INC.
Waterfront Plaza, Suite 1110
325 West Main Street
Louisville, KY 40202
(502) 585-4649

Contact: C. Dennis Riggs, President
Restrictions: Residents of the greater Louisville, KY, area
$ Given: Unavailable

NORTHERN KENTUCKY UNIVERSITY
Fireman's Dependent Scholarship
Administrative Center, 416 Nunn Drive
Highland Heights, KY 41099-7101
(606) 572-5144

Restrictions: Dependent or spouse of a disabled or deceased Kentucky fire fighter
$ Given: Unavailable

NORTHERN KENTUCKY UNIVERSITY
Scholarship for Commonwealth Scholars
Administrative Center, 416 Nunn Drive
Highland Heights, KY 41099-7101
(606) 572-5144

Restrictions: Freshman, Kentucky resident; minimum score of 23 on ACT
$ Given: Not available

JOHN B. AND BROWNIE YOUNG MEMORIAL FUND

c/o Owensboro National Bank, Trust Department
230 Frederica Street
Owensboro, KY 42301
(502) 926-3232

Restrictions: Students in school districts of Owensboro, Davies, and McClean counties, KY
$ Given: 84 grants of $4,500 each

LOUISIANA

BOARD OF TRUSTEES ACADEMIC AWARDS

Louisiana Tech University
P.O. Box 7925, Tech Station
Ruston, LA 71272
(318) 257-2641

Contact: Jan Albritton, Financial Officer
Restrictions: Students in good academic standing; ACT score of at least 26
$ Given: 13 awards of $1,200

THE WILLIAM T. AND ETHEL LEWIS BURTON FOUNDATION

1 Lake Shore Drive, Suite 1700
Lake Charles, LA 70629
(318) 433-0142

Contact: William B. Lawton, Chairman
Restrictions: Southwest Louisiana high school seniors
$ Given: $1,000 awards over four years

PAUL DOUGLAS
TEACHER SCHOLARSHIP
P.O. Box 91202
Baton Rouge, LA 70821
(504) 922-1038

Contact: Winona Kahoa, Scholarship Director
Restrictions: Louisiana residents who promise to teach for two years for each year of funding received; must have graduated in the top 10% of class with minimum 3.0 GPA and have a combined SAT score of 920 or minimum ACT score of 22
$ Given: Approximately 69 awards, range, $2,500–$5,000
   Deadline: April 15

FFA WAL-MART SCHOLARSHIP
P.O. Box 15160
Alexandria, VA 22309-0160
(703) 360-3600

Restrictions: FFA member; freshman-year agriculture major; resident of Alabama, Arkansas, Arizona, California, Colorado, Connecticut, Delaware, Florida, Georgia, Hawaii, Idaho, Illinois, Indiana, Iowa, Kansas, Kentucky, Louisiana, Maine, Maryland, Michigan, Minnesota, Mississippi, Missouri, Montana, Nebraska, Nevada, New Hampshire, New Mexico, New York, North Carolina, North Dakota, Ohio, Oklahoma, Oregon, Pennsylvania, Puerto Rico, Rhode Island, South Carolina, South Dakota, Tennessee, Texas, Utah, Virginia, Washington State, West Virginia, Wisconsin, or Wyoming
$ Given: Approximately 50 awards of $1,000
   Deadline: February 15

ED E. AND GLADYS HURLEY FOUNDATION
c/o Bank One
P.O. Box 21116
Shreveport, LA 71154
(318) 226-2110

Contact: Monette Holler
Restrictions: Loans to residents of Arizona, Louisiana, and Texas to attend institution of their choice

$ Given: Unavailable
Deadline: May 31

LOUISIANA OFFICE OF STUDENT FINANCIAL ASSISTANCE
P.O. Box 91202
Baton Rouge, LA 70821-9202
(504) 922-1011

Restrictions: Graduates of Louisiana high schools with GPA of 2.5 or above to attend a Louisiana state-supported institution
$ Given: 6,000 grants of $400; can be renewed for five years
Deadline: March 15

LOUISIANA OFFICE OF STUDENT FINANCIAL ASSISTANCE
Louisiana State Student Incentive Grant
P.O. Box 91202
Baton Rouge, LA 70821-9202
(504) 922-1011

Contact: Financial Aid Office of School student will attend
Restrictions: Louisiana residents attending Louisiana schools; financial need; minimum 2.0 GPA
$ Given: Grant range $200–$2,000
Deadline: March 15

LOUISIANA OFFICE OF STUDENT FINANCIAL ASSISTANCE
Louisiana Tuition Assistance Plan
P.O. Box 91202
Baton Rouge, LA 70821-9202
(504) 922-1011

Contact: Community Supervisor
Restrictions: High school seniors who are Louisiana residents pursuing an undergraduate degree or technical degree at a state Louisiana school
$ Given: Awards average $650–$2,500; renewable
Deadline: March 15

WILLIS AND MILDRED PELLERIN FOUNDATION
Leglue and Company
P.O. Box 400
Kenner, LA 70063-0400

Contact: Lynn Hotfelter, Administrative Assistant
Restrictions: U.S. citizens; four-year institution; residents of Louisiana to attend college or university in Louisiana; based on merit
$ Given: 100 grants; range, $300–$600
Deadline: February 1

USL FOUNDATION SCHOLARSHIPS

University of Southwestern Louisiana
East University Avenue
P.O. Box 44548
Lafayette, LA 70504
(318) 231-6515

Contact: Mrs. Gracie Guillory
Restrictions: Grants for students at USL
$ Given: Grants of various amounts

FRED B. AND RUTH B. ZIGLER FOUNDATION

P.O. Box 986
Jennings, LA 70546
(318) 824-2413

Contact: Marie Romero, Secretary-Treasurer
Restrictions: High school seniors of Jefferson Davis Parish, LA
$ Given: 23 grants of $10,000 over four years
Deadline: March 10

MAINE

MARJORIE SELLS CARTER TRUST BOY SCOUT SCHOLARSHIP

P.O. Box 527
West Chatham, MA 02669
(508) 945-1225

Contact: Mrs. B. J. Shaffer, Administrative Secretary
Restrictions: Applicant must be a Boy Scout from one of six (including Maine) New England states; have been active in scouting for two years; leadership ability and financial need

$ Given: Approximately 30 grants of $1,500 each
 Deadline: April 15

FFA WAL-MART SCHOLARSHIP

P.O. Box 15160
Alexandria, VA 22309-0160
(703) 360-3600

Restrictions: FFA member; freshman-year agriculture major; resident of Alabama, Arkansas, Arizona, California, Colorado, Connecticut, Delaware, Florida, Georgia, Hawaii, Idaho, Illinois, Indiana, Iowa, Kansas, Kentucky, Louisiana, Maine, Maryland, Michigan, Minnesota, Mississippi, Missouri, Montana, Nebraska, Nevada, New Hampshire, New Mexico, New York, North Carolina, North Dakota, Ohio, Oklahoma, Oregon, Pennsylvania, Puerto Rico, Rhode Island, South Carolina, South Dakota, Tennessee, Texas, Utah, Virginia, Washington State, West Virginia, Wisconsin, or Wyoming
$ Given: Approximately 50 awards of $1,000
 Deadline: February 15

FRED FORSYTHE EDUCATIONAL TRUST FUND

c/o Fleet Investment Services
P.O. Box 923
Exchange Street
Bangor, ME 04401
(207) 941-6000

Restrictions: Graduates of Bucksport High School, Maine
$ Given: Unavailable

CHET JORDAN LEADERSHIP AWARD

P.O. Box 574
Portland, ME 04112
(207) 667-9735

Contact: Joanne Foster
Restrictions: Maine high school graduate; exhibit family values and community service; academic or athletic excellence
$ Given: One award of $2,500
 Deadline: May 1

THE MAINE COMMUNITY FOUNDATION, INC.
245 Main Street
P.O. Box 148
Ellsworth, ME 04605
(207) 667-9735

Contact: Elizabeth Myrick
Restrictions: Residents of Maine
$ Given: Over 87 scholarship funds
  Deadline: Varies

MAINE STUDENT INCENTIVE SCHOLARSHIP
State House Station 119
Augusta, ME 04333
(800) 228-3734

Restrictions: Maine resident attending a participating school
$ Given: 9,200 awards, range, $500–$1,000
  Deadline: May 1

MAINE STUDENTS INCENTIVE SCHOLARSHIP PROGRAM
Financial Authority of Maine
119 State House Station
Augusta, ME 04330-0119

Contact: Rochelle Bridgham, Program Assistant
Restrictions: Maine residents attending eligible institutions; financial need
$ Given: Awards, range, $500–$1,000; renewable
  Deadline: May 1

EMILY K. ROAD SCHOLARSHIP
92 Raymond Road
Brunswick, ME 04011
(207) 725-1125

Contact: Joyce Chaplin
Restrictions: Cumberland, Oxford, or York county resident between the ages of 17 and 25

$ Given: Four awards, range, $500–$1,200
  Deadline: May 6

WILLIAM SEARLS SCHOLARSHIP FUND
c/o First National Bank of Bar Harbor
Box 258
Bar Harbor, ME 04609
(207) 288-3341

Restrictions: Residents of Southwest Harbor or Bar Harbor, Maine
$ Given: 40 grants; average, $350–$800
  Deadline: April 15

VETERANS DEPENDENTS EDUCATIONAL BENEFITS
State of Maine Division of Veterans Services
117 State House Station
Augusta, ME 04333-0117

Restrictions: Dependents under 22 or spouses of Maine veterans who were prisoners of war, MIA, or permenantly disabled; attend Maine school
$ Given: Not available

MARYLAND

DELEGATE SCHOLARSHIP
State Scholarship Administration
16 Francis Street
Annapolis, MD 21401-1781
(410) 974-5370

Contact: Gail Fisher, Program Administrator
Restrictions: Maryland resident attending Maryland school; applicant must contact all three delegates in their state legislation district on how to apply.
$ Given: Approximately 2,000 grants ranging from $200; full tuition and fees
  Deadline: Varies

PAUL DOUGLAS TEACHER SCHOLARSHIP

State Scholarship Administration
16 Francis Street
Annapolis, MD 21401-1781
(410) 974-5370

Contact: Michael Smith, Program Administrator
Restrictions: Maryland resident who is in top 10% of class; recipient must teach in Maryland school for two years for each year of assistance received.
$ Given: Approximately 59 awards of $5,000
Deadline: March 31

EDUCATIONAL ASSISTANCE GRANT

State Scholarship Administration
16 Francis Street
Annapolis, MD 21401-1781
(410) 974-5370

Restrictions: Maryland resident attending Maryland school full-time; financial need
$ Given: Approximately 14,000 awards, range, $200–$3,000
Deadline: March 1

FFA WAL-MART SCHOLARSHIP

P.O. Box 15160
Alexandria, VA 22309-0160
(703) 360-3600

Restrictions: FFA member; freshman-year agriculture major; resident of Alabama, Arkansas, Arizona, California, Colorado, Connecticut, Delaware, Florida, Georgia, Hawaii, Idaho, Illinois, Indiana, Iowa, Kansas, Kentucky, Louisiana, Maine, Maryland, Michigan, Minnesota, Mississippi, Missouri, Montana, Nebraska, Nevada, New Hampshire, New Mexico, New York, North Carolina, North Dakota, Ohio, Oklahoma, Oregon, Pennsylvania, Puerto Rico, Rhode Island, South Carolina, South Dakota, Tennessee, Texas, Utah, Virginia, Washington State, West Virginia, Wisconsin, or Wyoming
$ Given: Approximately 50 awards of $1,000
Deadline: February 15

GUARANTEED ACCESS GRANT PROGRAM
State Scholarship Administration
16 Francis Street
Annapolis, MD 21401-1781
(410) 974-5370

Restrictions: Maryland residents attending school full time; under 22; financial need; minimum 2.5 GPA
$ Given: Up to $8,000 per year

LOATS FOUNDATION
c/o Evangelical Lutheran Church
35 East Church Street
Frederick City, MD 21701
(301) 663-6361

Contact: Reverend Philip Fogerty
Restrictions: Residents of Frederick County, MD; financial need
$ Given: Range, $750–$1,000

MARYLAND STATE SCHOLARSHIP ADMINISTRATION
Maryland Distinguished Scholar Award
Jeffrey Building
16 Francis Street
Annapolis, MD 21401-1781
(410) 974-5370

Restrictions: Graduate of, or senior at, a Maryland high school and legal resident of Maryland; 3.7–4.0 GPA or semifinalist in National Merit Scholarship competition; also, five awards in the arts
$ Given: 350 awards of $3,000 per year, renewable for three years
    Deadline: February 15

MARYLAND STATE SCHOLARSHIP ADMINISTRATION
Maryland Senatorial Scholarships, General State Program
Jeffrey Building
16 Francis Street
Annapolis, MD 21401-1781
(410) 974-5370

Contact: Lula Caldwell, Administrative Assistant

Restrictions: Resident students attending institutions in Maryland; U.S. citizenship or legal residency
$ Given: Unspecified number of $200–$2,000 grants; renewable if you maintain a B average
Deadlines: Apply between January 1 and March 1

NATIONAL BASKETBALL ASSOCIATION

Washington Bullets Scholarship
Washington Bullets
Capital Centre
Landover, MD 20785
(301) 773-2255

Contact: Rick Moreland, Director of Public Relations
Restrictions: Residents of the area within 75 miles of the Capital Centre; scholastic standing (GPA, SAT 1 or ACT scores) and essay response
$ Given: Two grants for $1,000 each
Deadline: March 1

PRINCE GEORGE'S CHAMBER OF COMMERCE FOUNDATION SCHOLARSHIP

Prince George's Chamber of Commerce
4640 Forbes Boulevard
Suite 200
Lanham, MD 20706
(301) 731-5000

Contact: Robert Zinsmeister
Restrictions: Residents of Prince George's County, MD, who have graduated from county schools; preference to business-related majors; financial need
$ Given: 17 awards annually; range, $1,000–$2,760
Deadline: May 15

J. C. STEWART MEMORIAL TRUST

7718 Finns Lane
Lanham, MD 20706
(301) 459-4200

Contact: Robert S. Hoyert, Trustee

Restrictions: Residents of Maryland
$ Given: 15–20 grants of $3,000
$ Loaned: Loans up to $4,000
 Deadline: Grants, September 1; Loans July 1

MASSACHUSETTS

ADAMS SCHOLARSHIP FUND
c/o First National Bank of Boston
99 West Street
Pittsfield, MA 01201
(413) 499-3000

Contact: Linda Casella
Restrictions: Residents of Adams-Cheshire, MA, Regional School District
$ Given: Unavailable
 Deadline: April 1

WALTER S. BARR SCHOLARSHIP
1441 Main Street
Box 3034
Springfield, MA 01102
(413) 739-4222

Restrictions: Residents of Hampden County, MA
$ Given: $1,000 per year; renewable
 Deadline: December 31

THE THEODORE H. BARTH FOUNDATION, INC.
630 Fifth Avenue, Suite 2000
New York, NY 10111
(212) 332-3466

Contact: Irving P. Berelson, Vice President
Restrictions: High school graduates of Wareham, MA, School District
$ Given: Unavailable

BRANDEIS UNIVERSITY COMMUNITY SERVICE AWARD

415 South Street
Waltham, MA 02254-9110
(617) 736-3700

Contact: Peter Guimette, Director of Financial Aid
Restrictions: Scholarships for local/state students with merit
$ Given: Unavailable

FLORENCE EVANS BUSHEE FOUNDATION, INC.

Palmer and Dodge
One Beacon Street
Boston, MA 02108
(617) 573-0100

Contact: Louise Pierce, Secretary
Restrictions: College students who are residents of Newburyport, MA, Newbury, Byfield, and Rowley
$ Given: 118 grants totaling $110,050
   Deadline: May 1

MARJORIE SELLS CARTER TRUST
BOY SCOUT SCHOLARSHIP

P.O. Box 527
West Chatham, MA 02669
(508) 945-1225

Contact: Mrs. B. J. Shaffer, Administrative Secretary
Restrictions: Boy Scout from one of the six New England states (including Massachusetts). Must have been active in scouting for at least two years; leadership ability; financial need
$ Given: Approximately 35 awards averaging $1,500
   Deadline: April 15

THE JAMES W. COLGAN FUND

c/o Fleet Bank, Trust Department
1 Monarch Place
Springfield, MA 01144
(413) 787-8524

Contact: Delores Braza, Trust Officer
Restrictions: Residents of Massachusetts for at least five years
$ Loaned: Average award, $1,000
   Deadline: April 15

EDWARDS SCHOLARSHIP FUND

10 Post Office Square South
Suite 1230
Boston, MA 02109
(617) 426-4434

Contact: Brenda McCarthy
Restrictions: Residents of Boston, MA, since junior year; under age 25
$ Loaned: Range, $250–$5,000
   Deadline: March 1

FRIENDSHIP FUND, INC.

c/o Boston Safe Deposit and Trust Company
1 Boston Place
Boston, MA 02108
(617) 722-7772

Restrictions: Students and Massachusetts residents who are nominated by members of the fund
$ Given: Unavailable
   Deadline: May 31

GILBERT GRANT

Massachusetts Office of Student Financial Assistance
330 Stuart Street
Boston, MA 02116

Restrictions: Massachusetts residents attending Massachusetts schools full time
$ Given: Range, $200–$2,500

CHRISTIAN A. HERTER MEMORIAL SCHOLARSHIP

Office of Student Financial Assistance
330 Stuart Street
Boston, MA 02116
(617) 727-9420

Contact: Cynthia M. Gray, Scholarship Officer
Restrictions: Massachusetts resident who has experienced personal hardship or medical problem or overcome a personal obstacle
$ Given: Approximately 24 awards averaging $9,000
Deadline: March 31

EDWARD BANGS KELLEY AND ELZA KELLEY FOUNDATION, INC.

243 South Street, P.O. Drawer M
Hyannis, MA 02601
(508) 775-3117

Contact: Henry L. Murphy, Jr., President
Restrictions: Barnstable County, MA, residents
$ Given: Unavailable
Deadline: April 30

WILLIAM E. MALONEY FOUNDATION

P.O. Box 515
Lexington, MA 02173
(617) 860-7313

Restrictions: Residents of Massachusetts
$ Given: Three grants totaling $15,500
Deadline: Rotating

MASSACHUSETTS OFFICE OF STUDENT FINANCIAL ASSISTANCE

General Scholarship Program
330 Stuart Street
Boston, MA 02116
(617) 727-9420

Restrictions: Permanent Massachusetts residents for study at an independent accredited institution; financial need
$ Given: Unspecified number of grants of $200–$2,500
Deadline: May 1

MASSACHUSETTS OFFICE OF STUDENT FINANCIAL ASSISTANCE

Public Service Scholarship
330 Stuart Street
Boston, MA 02116
(617) 727-9420

Contact: Jill McTague
Restrictions: Permanent Massachusetts resident enrolled in a full-time program at a public Massachusetts institution; parent who died in the line of duty as a fire, police, or correction officer
$ Given: Unspecified number of full tuition grants
   Deadline: March 1

MASSACHUSETTS STATE SCHOLARSHIP PROGRAM
OFFICE OF STUDENT FINANCIAL ASSISTANCE
330 Stuart Street
Boston, MA 02116
(617) 727-9420

Contact: Clantha Carrigan McCurdy
Restrictions: Massachusetts resident; full-time student; financial need
$ Given: Range, $250–$2,500
   Deadline: May 1

JAMES Z. NAURISON SCHOLARSHIP FUND
c/o Fleet Bank
P.O. Box 9003
Springfield, MA 01102-9003
(413) 787-8524

Restrictions: Students from Hampden, Hampshire, Franklin, and Berkshire counties, MA; and towns of Enfield and Suffield, CT
$ Given: Varies
   Deadline: April 15

HORACE SMITH FUND
1441 Main Street
Box 3034
Springfield, MA 01102
(413) 739-4222

Restrictions: Residents of and attended Hampden County, MA, high schools
$ Loaned: Unspecified number of $2,000 loans for new students
   Deadlines: June 15 loans; July 1 for high school seniors and college students

URANN FOUNDATION

P.O. Box 1788
Brockton, MA 02303
(508) 588-7744

Contact: Robert Le Boeuf, Administrator
Restrictions: Massachusetts residents whose families are engaged in the production of cranberries
$ Given: Average award $1,500
  Deadline: April 15

MICHIGAN

AMERICAN LEGION, DEPARTMENT OF MICHIGAN

Guy M. Wilson Scholarships
212 North Verlinden Street
Lansing, MI 48915

Restrictions: Michigan resident attending Michigan school; child of a veteran living or deceased
$ Given: 20 awards of $500
  Deadline: February 1

ANN ARBOR AREA COMMUNITY FOUNDATION

201 South Main Street, Suite 801
Ann Arbor, MI 48104
(313) 663-0401

Contact: Washtenaw and Cleary colleges
Restrictions: Residents of Ann Arbor, MI, attending Washtenaw County College and Cleary College
$ Given: Unavailable

C. K. EDDY FAMILY MEMORIAL FUND

Citizen's Bank
101 North Washington Avenue
Saginaw, MI 48607
(517) 776-7200

Contact: Bonnie Black
Restrictions: Residents of Saginaw County, MI, for minimum
one year prior to application
$ Loaned: Loans totaling $196,372
    Deadline: May 1

H. T. EWALD FOUNDATION
15175 East Jefferson Avenue
Grosse Pointe Park, MI 48230
(313) 821-2000

Restrictions: High school seniors who are residents
of the metropolitan Detroit, MI, area
$ Given: 12–18 grants; range, $500–$3,000;
total varies with available funds
    Deadline: April 1

FFA WAL-MART SCHOLARSHIP
P.O. Box 15160
Alexandria, VA 22309-0160
(703) 360-3600

Restrictions: FFA member; freshman-year agriculture major; resident of
Alabama, Arkansas, Arizona, California, Colorado, Connecticut,
Delaware, Florida, Georgia, Hawaii, Idaho, Illinois, Indiana, Iowa, Kansas,
Kentucky, Louisiana, Maine, Maryland, Michigan, Minnesota, Mississippi,
Missouri, Montana, Nebraska, Nevada, New Hampshire, New Mexico,
New York, North Carolina, North Dakota, Ohio, Oklahoma, Oregon,
Pennsylvania, Puerto Rico, Rhode Island, South Carolina, South Dakota,
Tennessee, Texas, Utah, Virginia, Washington State, West Virginia, Wis-
consin, or Wyoming
$ Given: Approximately 50 awards of $1,000
    Deadline: February 15

GRAND HAVEN AREA COMMUNITY FOUNDATION, INC.
One South Harbor, Suite 3
Grand Haven, MI 49417
(616) 842-6378

Contact: Nancy Riekse, Foundation Director

Restrictions: Residents of Grand Haven, Spring Lake, and Ferrgysburg, and northwest Ottawa County, MI; academic achievement and/or financial need
$ Given: 30 scholarships; average award $1,500
   Deadline: March 1

GRAND RAPIDS FOUNDATION

161 Ottawa, Northwest
Suite 209C
Grand Rapids, MI 49503
(616) 454-1751

Contact: Laurie Craft
Restrictions: Residents of Kent County, MI, and students attending Lowell, Holland, and Belding high schools
$ Given: Range, $500–$2,500
   Deadline: April 3

GEORGE W. AND SADIE MARIE JUHL SCHOLARSHIP FUND

c/o Southern Michigan Bank and Trust
51 West Pearl Street
Coldwater, MI 49036
(517) 279-7511

Contact: Margo Brush
Restrictions: Residents of Branch County, MI, or local high schools/colleges to attend colleges and universities in Michigan; financial need
$ Given: Grant range, starting at $2,000

KENT MEDICAL FOUNDATION

1400 Michigan Northeast
Grand Rapids, MI 49503
(616) 458-4157

Contact: William G. McClimans, Executive Director
Restrictions: Residents of Kent, MI, and bordering counties, for education in medicine, nursing, and related health fields; must attend local college
$ Given: Four grants, each for $500
   Deadline: April 1

MCCURDY MEMORIAL SCHOLARSHIP FOUNDATION
Wagner and Jordan Law Offices
134 West Van Buren
Battle Creek, MI 49017
(616) 962-9591

Contact: Michael C. Jordan, Attorney
Restrictions: Calhoun County, MI, residents
$ Given: 23 grants; range, $500–$1,000
   Deadline: March 31

EDWIN T. MEREDITH FOUNDATION

Contact: Local County 4-H Office or State 4-H Office
Restrictions: Must be a 4-H member for at least one year; outstanding achievement; resident of Illinois, Indiana, Iowa, Kansas, Michigan, Minnesota, Missouri, Nebraska, New York, North Dakota, Ohio, Oklahoma, Pennsylvania, South Dakota, or Wisconsin
$ Given: Approximately three awards of $1,000
   Deadline: September 1

MICHIGAN ADULT PART-TIME GRANTS
Michigan Higher Education Assistance Authority
P.O. Box 30466
Lansing, MI 48909-7966
(800) 877-5659

Restrictions: Michigan students enrolled part-time at Michigan schools; financial need
$ Given: $600

MICHIGAN DEPARTMENT OF EDUCATION
Office of Scholarships and Grants
Michigan Higher Education Assistance Authority
P.O. Box 30462
Lansing, MI 48909-7962
(517) 373-3394

Restrictions: Residents of Michigan not less than five years; submit ACT scores; financial need; for full-time undergraduate study at an eligible Michigan college or university; U.S. citizenship

$ Given: Unspecified number of $100–$1,200 grants, renewable
Deadlines: February 21 for high school seniors; March 21 for college students

MICHIGAN DEPARTMENT OF EDUCATION

Michigan Tuition Grants
Student Financial Assistance Services
P.O. Box 30462
Lansing, MI 48909-7962
(517) 373-3394

Restrictions: Residents of Michigan who are full-time students at independent nonprofit colleges and universities in Michigan; financial need
$ Given: Unspecified number of $100–$1,300 grants, renewable
Deadline: Varies

MICHIGAN EDUCATIONAL OPPORTUNITY GRANT

Michigan Higher Education Assistance Authority
P.O. Box 30466
Lansing, MI 48909-7966
(800) 877-5659

Restrictions: Michigan residents attending state schools; financial need
$ Given: $1,000

MUSKEGON COUNTY COMMUNITY FOUNDATION, INC.

Frauenthal Building, Suite 200
425 West Western Avenue
Muskegon, MI 49440
(616) 722-4538

Restrictions: Muskegon County, MI, residents only
$ Given: 250 grants; range, $300–$2,500
Deadline: March 15

JOHN W. AND ROSE E. WATSON FOUNDATION

5800 Weiss Street
Saginaw, MI 48603
(517) 797-6633

Contact: Jean Seman, Secretary

Restrictions: Residents of Saginaw, MI, graduating from Catholic high schools
$ Given: Maximum of 115 grants of $1,200 (average)
   Deadline: April 1

WINSHIP MEMORIAL SCHOLARSHIP FOUNDATION
c/o Comerica Bank-Battle Creek, Trust Division
25 West Michigan Mall
Battle Creek, MI 49017
(616) 966-6340

Contact: Marcia Owen, Executive Director
Restrictions: Graduates of Battle Creek, MI, area public high schools
$ Given: 35 grants; range, $800–$2,500
   Deadline: March 1

MINNESOTA

FFA WAL-MART SCHOLARSHIP
P.O. Box 15160
Alexandria, VA 22309-0160
(703) 360-3600

Restrictions: FFA member; freshman-year agriculture major; resident of Alabama, Arkansas, Arizona, California, Colorado, Connecticut, Delaware, Florida, Georgia, Hawaii, Idaho, Illinois, Indiana, Iowa, Kansas, Kentucky, Louisiana, Maine, Maryland, Michigan, Minnesota, Mississippi, Missouri, Montana, Nebraska, Nevada, New Hampshire, New Mexico, New York, North Carolina, North Dakota, Ohio, Oklahoma, Oregon, Pennsylvania, Puerto Rico, Rhode Island, South Carolina, South Dakota, Tennessee, Texas, Utah, Virginia, Washington State, West Virginia, Wisconsin, or Wyoming
$ Given: Approximately 50 awards of $1,000
   Deadline: February 15

CLEM JAUNICH EDUCATION TRUST
5353 Gamble Drive, Suite 110
Minneapolis, MN, 55416
(612) 546-1555

Contact: Joseph L. Abrahamson, Trustee
Restrictions: Attended high school in Delano, MN, or live within seven-mile radius and/or live in Wright County and plan to attend premedical or preseminary school
$ Given: Seven grants; range, $250–$1,250
   Deadline: July 1

EDWIN T. MEREDITH FOUNDATION

Contact: Local County 4-H Office or State 4-H Office
Restrictions: Must be a 4-H member for at least one year; outstanding achievement; resident of Illinois, Indiana, Iowa, Kansas, Michigan, Minnesota, Missouri, Nebraska, New York, North Dakota, Ohio, Oklahoma, Pennsylvania, South Dakota, or Wisconsin
$ Given: Approximately three awards of $1,000
   Deadline: September 1

MINNESOTA HIGHER EDUCATION COORDINATING BOARD

Student Loan Program
550 Cedar Street, Suite 400
Capitol Square Building
St. Paul, MN 55101
(612) 296-3974

Restrictions: Residents of Minnesota, or nonresidents attending Minnesota institutions; financial need; U.S. citizenship or legal residency
$ Loaned: 11,000 loans of up to $4,000 per year
   Deadline: None

MINNESOTA HIGHER EDUCATION SERVICES OFFICE

Scholarship and Grant Program
550 Cedar Street, Suite 400
Capitol Square Building
St. Paul, MN 55101
(612) 296-3974

Restrictions: Residents of Minnesota attending Minnesota institutions; U.S. citizenship or legal residency; financial need
$ Given: 57,000 grants; range, $300–$5,932
   Deadline: June 30

POTLATCH FOUNDATION
FOR HIGHER EDUCATION SCHOLARSHIP
P.O. Box 193591
San Francisco, CA 94119-3591
(415) 576-8829

Contact: Jenni Rogers
Restrictions: Must live or attend high school within 30 miles of a major Potlatch facility; academic achievement; financial need; leadership ability
$ Given: Approximately 80 awards of $1,400
   Deadline: February 15

TOZER FOUNDATION, INC.
U.S. Bank Trust
SFPSO 200
322 Minnesota
St. Paul, MN 55164-0701
(612) 244-0904

Contact: Elizabeth Keyes
Restrictions: Residents of three Minnesota counties
$ Given: Number and amount of grants vary

WASIE FOUNDATION SCHOLARSHIP
Wasie Foundation
U.S. Bank Place, Suite 4700
601 Second Avenue South
Minneapolis, MN 55402
(612) 332-3883

Contact: Leah Johnson, scholarship administrator
Restrictions: Christian students of Polish ancestry attending full-time specified Minnesota institutions; financial need; academic ability; extracurricular activities; personal qualities; members of the Communist Party not eligible
$ Given: 50 awards; amount varies with student's need; range, $500–$3,500
   Deadline: April 15

MISSISSIPPI

FFA WAL-MART SCHOLARSHIP

P.O. Box 15160
Alexandria, VA 22309-0160
(703) 360-3600

Restrictions: FFA member; freshman-year agriculture major; resident of Alabama, Arkansas, Arizona, California, Colorado, Connecticut, Delaware, Florida, Georgia, Hawaii, Idaho, Illinois, Indiana, Iowa, Kansas, Kentucky, Louisiana, Maine, Maryland, Michigan, Minnesota, Mississippi, Missouri, Montana, Nebraska, Nevada, New Hampshire, New Mexico, New York, North Carolina, North Dakota, Ohio, Oklahoma, Oregon, Pennsylvania, Puerto Rico, Rhode Island, South Carolina, South Dakota, Tennessee, Texas, Utah, Virginia, Washington State, West Virginia, Wisconsin, or Wyoming
$ Given: Approximately 50 awards of $1,000
   Deadline: February 15

FIELD COOPERATIVE ASSOCIATION, INC.

P.O. Box 5054
Jackson, MS 39296
(601) 939-9295

Contact: Ginger Chill
Restrictions: Residents of Mississippi
$ Loaned: $500,000–$600,000 per year; $3,000/year; $9,000 over three years per student
   Deadline: Year-round

JUNIOR MISS AWARD

Mississippi University for Women
Box W-1614
Columbus, MS 39701
(601) 329-7114

Contact: Mr. Wyckoff
$ Given: $750 per year, renewable

LAW ENFORCEMENT OFFICERS AND FIREMAN
Scholarship Program
3825 Ridgewood Road
Jackson, MS 39211-6453
(601) 982-6663

Restrictions: Spouse or child of a full-time Mississippi law enforcement officer or firefighter who was killed or permanently disabled in the line of duty; recipient must attend a state Mississippi school.
$ Given: Tuition, fees, and dorm fees

STATE STUDENT INCENTIVE GRANT
State Institutions of Higher Learning
3825 Ridgewood Road
Jackson, MS 39211-6453

Restrictions: Mississippi residents studying full time at a Mississippi school; financial need
$ Given: Range, $100–$1,500 per year

JOHN M. WILL MEMORIAL SCHOLARSHIP FOUNDATION
Mobile Chapter of the Society
of Professional Journalists
P.O. Box 290
Mobile, AL 36601-0290

Contact: William Steele Holman II
Restrictions: Residents of George and Jackson counties, Mississippi, studying journalism
$ Given: $3,500
  Deadline: March 22

WILLIAM F. WINTER TEACHER SCHOLAR LOAN PROGRAM
State Institutions of Higher Learning
3825 Ridgewood Road
Jackson, MS 39211-6453

Restrictions: Student agrees to teach for one year for each year of money awarded; must maintain a 2.5 GPA
$ Given: Range, $1,000–$3,000 per year
  Deadline: June 15

MISSOURI

MARGUERITE ROSS BARNETT MEMORIAL SCHOLARSHIP
P.O. Box 6730
Jefferson City, MO 65102
(573) 751-3940

Restrictions: Must attend school at least half-time and work a minimum of 20 hours per week
$ Given: Up to $2,200 per award

BOUR MEMORIAL SCHOLARSHIP TRUST
P.O. Box 38
Kansas City, MO 64141

Contact: David Ross
Nation's Bank
1016 Main Street
Lexington, MO 64067
(660) 259-4661

Restrictions: Graduates of Lafayette County, MO, high schools to attend college of their choice; financial need required
$ Given: Varies
   Deadline: April 1

ROBERT C. BYRD HONORS SCHOLARSHIP
P.O. Box 480
Jefferson City, MO 65102
(573) 751-2931

Contact: Celeste Ferguson
Restrictions: Missouri resident freshman rank in top 10% of class; score in top 10% of ACT; show proof of registration with Selective Service
$ Given: Average grant $1,500
   Deadline: March 31

JAMES A. AND JULIET L. DAVIS FOUNDATION, INC.
418 First National Center
P.O. Box 2027
Hutchinson, KA 67504-2027
(316) 663-5021

Contact: Carol Shaft, Secretary
Restrictions: Hutchinson high school committee choice of graduates attending college in Kansas or Missouri
$ Given: Range, $2,500–$5,000

FFA WAL-MART SCHOLARSHIP

P.O. Box 15160
Alexandria, VA 22309-0160
(703) 360-3600

Restrictions: FFA member; freshman-year agriculture major; resident of Alabama, Arkansas, Arizona, California, Colorado, Connecticut, Delaware, Florida, Georgia, Hawaii, Idaho, Illinois, Indiana, Iowa, Kansas, Kentucky, Louisiana, Maine, Maryland, Michigan, Minnesota, Mississippi, Missouri, Montana, Nebraska, Nevada, New Hampshire, New Mexico, New York, North Carolina, North Dakota, Ohio, Oklahoma, Oregon, Pennsylvania, Puerto Rico, Rhode Island, South Carolina, South Dakota, Tennessee, Texas, Utah, Virginia, Washington State, West Virginia, Wisconsin, or Wyoming
$ Given: Approximately 50 awards of $1,000
Deadline: February 15

MAY H. ILGENFRITZ TESTAMENTARY TRUST

P.O. Box 311
Sedalia, MO 65302-0311
(660) 826-3310

Contact: Guidance Officer, Smith-Cotton High School
Restrictions: Sedalia, MO, residents; may attend college anywhere
$ Given: Grant numbers and amounts vary.

EDWIN T. MEREDITH FOUNDATION

Contact: Local County 4-H Office or State 4-H Office
Restrictions: Must be a 4-H member for at least one year; outstanding achievement; resident of Illinois, Indiana, Iowa, Kansas, Michigan, Minnesota, Missouri, Nebraska, New York, North Dakota, Ohio, Oklahoma, Pennsylvania, South Dakota, or Wisconsin

$ Given: Approximately three awards of $1,000
  Deadline: September 1

MISSOURI COORDINATING BOARD
FOR HIGHER EDUCATION
Higher Education Academic Scholarship Program
3515 Amazonas Drive
Jefferson City, MO 65109
(314) 751-3940

Restrictions: Missouri residents enrolled in or attending Missouri institutions full time; top 3% of composite ACT/SAT scores for Missouri high schools; U.S. citizen or permanent resident
$ **Given:**   6,000 to 6,400 grants of $2,000; renewable
  Deadline: July 31

MISSOURI TEACHER
EDUCATION SCHOLARSHIP
Missouri Department of Elementary and Secondary Education
P.O. Box 480
Jefferson City, MO 65102-0480
(573) 751-4212

Restrictions: Missouri high school seniors, college freshmen, or sophomores in an approved teacher training program at a Missouri school; must rank in top 15% of either high school class or of scores on ACT or SAT.
$ **Given:** $ 2,000
  Deadline: February 15

MISSOURI COORDINATING BOARD
FOR HIGHER EDUCATION
Missouri Student Grant Program
3515 Amazonas Drive
Jefferson City, MO 65109
(314) 751-3940

Restrictions: Missouri residents; attending approved Missouri institution full-time; financial need required
$ **Given:**   Number of grants varies; $1,500 maximum amount
  Deadline: April 1

MONTANA

CHARLES M. BAIR MEMORIAL TRUST
U.S. Bank Trust National Association, MT
P.O. Box 30678
Billings, MT 59115
(406) 657-8127

Contact: Helen Hancock
Restrictions: Graduates of Meagher and Wheatland counties, Harlowtown High School, and White Sulphur Springs High School, Montana
$ Given: Full-tuition grants, eight awards given
   Deadline: March 15

DODD AND DOROTHY L. BRYAN FOUNDATION
P.O. Box 6287
Sheridan, WY 82801
(307) 672-3535

Contact: Rose Marie Madia, Manager
Restrictions: Residents of Sheridan, Campbell, and Johnson counties, WY, and of Powder River, Rosebud, and Big Horn counties, MT, with academic merit
$ Loaned: Loans of $4,000 per year, renewable
   Deadline: June 15

PAUL DOUGLAS TEACHER SCHOLARSHIP
University of Montana
33 South Last Chance Gulch
Helena, MT 59620
(406) 444-6954

Contact: Bill Lanan, Director of Montana Guaranteed Student Loan Program
Restrictions: Montana resident enrolled in teaching program grades K–12; rank in top 10% of high school class
$ Given: Approximately 10 $5,000 awards

FFA WAL-MART SCHOLARSHIP

P.O. Box 15160
Alexandria, VA 22309-0160
(703) 360-3600

Restrictions: FFA member; freshman-year agriculture major; resident of Alabama, Arkansas, Arizona, California, Colorado, Connecticut, Delaware, Florida, Georgia, Hawaii, Idaho, Illinois, Indiana, Iowa, Kansas, Kentucky, Louisiana, Maine, Maryland, Michigan, Minnesota, Mississippi, Missouri, Montana, Nebraska, Nevada, New Hampshire, New Mexico, New York, North Carolina, North Dakota, Ohio, Oklahoma, Oregon, Pennsylvania, Puerto Rico, Rhode Island, South Carolina, South Dakota, Tennessee, Texas, Utah, Virginia, Washington State, West Virginia, Wisconsin, or Wyoming
$ Given: Approximately 50 awards of $1,000
   Deadline: February 15

PACIFIC PRINTING AND IMAGING ASSOCIATION

Educational Trust Scholarships
180 Nickerson, Suite 102
Seattle, WA 98109

Contact: Jim Olsen
Restrictions: Students studying printing, print management, or graphic arts technology. Must live in Washington, Oregon, Arkansas, Idaho, Montana, or Hawaii
$ Given: 12 awards, range, $500–$2,500; renewable
   Deadline: April 1

TREACY COMPANY

Box 1700
Helena, MT 59624-1700
(406) 442-3632

Contact: James O'Connell
Restrictions: Residents of (freshman or sophomore years) Idaho, Montana, North Dakota, and South Dakota
$ Given: 25 to 35 grants of varying amounts; average $400
   Deadline: June 15

NEBRASKA

FFA WAL-MART SCHOLARSHIP

P.O. Box 15160
Alexandria, VA 22309-0160
(703) 360-3600

Restrictions: FFA member; freshman-year agriculture major; resident of Alabama, Arkansas, Arizona, California, Colorado, Connecticut, Delaware, Florida, Georgia, Hawaii, Idaho, Illinois, Indiana, Iowa, Kansas, Kentucky, Louisiana, Maine, Maryland, Michigan, Minnesota, Mississippi, Missouri, Montana, Nebraska, Nevada, New Hampshire, New Mexico, New York, North Carolina, North Dakota, Ohio, Oklahoma, Oregon, Pennsylvania, Puerto Rico, Rhode Island, South Carolina, South Dakota, Tennessee, Texas, Utah, Virginia, Washington State, West Virginia, Wisconsin, or Wyoming
$ Given: Approximately 50 awards of $1,000
　Deadline: February 15

MAYNARD JENSON AMERICAN LEGION

Memorial Scholarship
P.O. Box 5205
Lincoln, NE 68505
(402) 464-6338

Restrictions: Nebraska residents who are children or grandchildren of American Legion member or of a deceased veteran; must attend a Nebraska school
$ Given: Approximately eight awards of $500 each
　Deadline: March 1

EDWIN T. MEREDITH FOUNDATION

Contact: Local County 4-H Office or State 4-H Office
Restrictions: Must be a 4-H member for at least one year; outstanding achievement; resident of Illinois, Indiana, Iowa, Kansas, Michigan, Minnesota, Missouri, Nebraska, New York, North Dakota, Ohio, Oklahoma, Pennsylvania, South Dakota, or Wisconsin
$ Given: Approximately three awards of $1,000
　Deadline: September 1

NEBRASKA SCHOLARSHIP ASSISTANCE PROGRAM

Postsecondary Education Commission
P.O. Box 95005
Lincoln, NE 68509-9500

Restrictions: Nebraska residents attending Nebraska schools who have received Pell grants
$ Given: Award amounts determined by individual schools

NEBRASKA STATE SCHOLARSHIP AWARD PROGRAM

Postsecondary Education Commission
P.O. Box 95005
Lincoln, NE 68509-9500

Restrictions: Pell grant recipients attending Nebraska schools
$ Given: Award amounts determined by individual schools

NUCOR FOUNDATION, INC.

2100 Rexford Road
Charlotte, NC 28211
(704) 366-7000

Contact: Elizabeth Wells
Restrictions: Children of Nucor employees only; must maintain 2.0 GPA in college
$ Given: Up to $2,200 per year for four years
   Deadline: March 1

NEVADA

RICHARD AND JESSIE BARRINGTON
EDUCATIONAL FUND

c/o Wells Fargo Bank
343 Sausane Street, Third Floor
San Francisco, CA 94163

Contact: Ms. Sherry Smokey, Educational Coordinator, Washoe Tribe of Nevada and California Education Dept.

919 Highway 395 South
Gardnerville, NV 89410
(702) 265-4191
Restrictions: Enrolled members of Washoe Tribe
$ Given: One to three grants; range, $800–$2,000
  Deadlines: August 15, December 15

FFA WAL-MART SCHOLARSHIP
P.O. Box 15160
Alexandria, VA 22309-0160
(703) 360-3600

Restrictions: FFA member; freshman-year agriculture major; resident of Alabama, Arkansas, Arizona, California, Colorado, Connecticut, Delaware, Florida, Georgia, Hawaii, Idaho, Illinois, Indiana, Iowa, Kansas, Kentucky, Louisiana, Maine, Maryland, Michigan, Minnesota, Mississippi, Missouri, Montana, Nebraska, Nevada, New Hampshire, New Mexico, New York, North Carolina, North Dakota, Ohio, Oklahoma, Oregon, Pennsylvania, Puerto Rico, Rhode Island, South Carolina, South Dakota, Tennessee, Texas, Utah, Virginia, Washington State, West Virginia, Wisconsin, or Wyoming
$ Given: Approximately 50 awards of $1,000
  Deadline: February 15

NEVADA STUDENT INCENTIVE GRANT PROGRAM
2601 Enterprise Road
Reno, NV 29512
(702) 784-4666

Contact: Applications through financial aid office at institution of choice
Restrictions: Residents of Nevada attending Nevada institutions; must demonstrate financial need
$ Given: Range, $200–$5,000

POTLATCH FOUNDATION FOR
HIGHER EDUCATION SCHOLARSHIP
P.O. Box 193591
San Francisco, CA 94119-3591
(415) 576-8829

Contact: Jenni Rogers
Restrictions: Must live or attend high school within 30 miles of a major Potlatch facility; academic achievement; financial need; leadership ability
$ Given: Approximately 80 awards of $1,400
  Deadline: February 15

NEW HAMPSHIRE

AMERICAN LEGION-NEW HAMPSHIRE

Department of New Hampshire Scholarship
Department Adjutant
State House Annex
Concord, NH 03301
(603) 271-2211

Restrictions: New Hampshire high school graduates pursuing higher education; minimum three years state residency
$ Given: Five grants for $1,000 each
  Deadline: May 1

MARION J. BAGLEY SCHOLARSHIP

25 Capital Street, Room 29
Concord, NH 03301

Restrictions: New Hampshire resident
$ Given: Average $1,000 each
  Deadline: May 1

MARJORIE SELLS CARTER TRUST

P.O. Box 527
West Chatham, MA 02669
(508) 945-1225

Contact: Mrs. B.J. Shaffer
Restrictions: Boy Scout from one of the six New England states (including New Hampshire) who has been active in scouting for at least two years; leadership ability; financial need

$ Given: Approximately 35 awards, averaging $1,500
   Deadline: April 15

DEPARTMENT OF NEW HAMPSHIRE SCHOLARSHIP

State House Annex
Concord, NH 03301
(603) 271-2211

Contact: Herbert J. Geary
Restrictions: Freshman; graduate of a New Hampshire high school;
New Hampshire resident for at least three years
$ Given: Two $1,000 awards
   Deadline: May 1

FFA WAL-MART SCHOLARSHIP

P.O. Box 15160
Alexandria, VA 22309-0160
(703) 360-3600

Restrictions: FFA member; freshman-year agriculture major; resident of
Alabama, Arkansas, Arizona, California, Colorado, Connecticut,
Delaware, Florida, Georgia, Hawaii, Idaho, Illinois, Indiana, Iowa, Kansas,
Kentucky, Louisiana, Maine, Maryland, Michigan, Minnesota, Mississippi,
Missouri, Montana, Nebraska, Nevada, New Hampshire, New Mexico,
New York, North Carolina, North Dakota, Ohio, Oklahoma, Oregon,
Pennsylvania, Puerto Rico, Rhode Island, South Carolina, South Dakota,
Tennessee, Texas, Utah, Virginia, Washington State, West Virginia, Wisconsin, or Wyoming
$ Given: Approximately 50 awards of $1,000
   Deadline: February 15

ABBIE M. GRIFFIN EDUCATIONAL FUND

c/o Robert S. Winer
P.O. Box 488
Nashua, NH 03061-0488
(603) 882-5157

Restrictions: Residents of Merrimack, NH
$ Given: Varies
   Deadline: May 1

NEW HAMPSHIRE CHARITABLE FUND

37 Pleasant Street
Concord, NH 03301-4005
(603) 225-6641 Fax (603) 225-1700

Contact: Judith Burrows, Director, Student Aid
Restrictions: Scholarship or loans given in New Hampshire; six trusts administrated by New Hampshire Charitable Fund, each with its own criteria; call contact above for details; U.S. citizenship
$ Given: 550 grants; range, $100–$2,500; average, $1,200

NEW HAMPSHIRE INCENTIVE PROGRAM

New Hampshire Post Secondary Education Commission
Two Industrial Park Drive
Concord, NH 03301-8512

Restrictions: New Hampshire residents attending a designated school in New England; financial need
$ Given: Range, $450–$1,000
    Deadline: May 1

NEW JERSEY

CAREER ADVANCEMENT AWARDS

New Jersey Institute of Technology
University Heights
Newark, NJ 07102
(973) 596-3100

Contact: Joanne Range
Restrictions: NJIT freshmen who are women and/or minority students
$ Given: 25 awards, average, $1,000

JEWISH FOUNDATION FOR EDUCATION
OF WOMEN SCHOLARSHIP

330 West 58th Street
New York, NY 10019
(212) 265-2565

Contact: Florence Wallach, Executive Director
Restrictions: Full-time students who live within a 50-mile radius of New York City (including New Jersey and Long Island); law or M.B.A. candidates not eligible
$ Given: Annual awards, range, $500–$3,500
     Deadline: January 31

LAWRENCE LUTTERMAN MEMORIAL SCHOLARSHIP

War Memorial Building
Trenton, NJ 08608
(609) 695-5418

Restrictions: Descendant of a member of the American Legion, Department of New Jersey; freshman year
$ Given: Approximately four $1,000 awards
     Deadline: February 15

MIDDLESEX COUNTY MEDICAL SOCIETY FOUNDATION, INC.

575 Cranbury Road B-7
East Brunswick, NJ 08816
(908) 257-6800

Contact: Mary Alice Bruno, Executive Secretary
Restrictions: Good academic standing; residents (five-year minimum) of Middlesex County, NJ, for study of medicine, nursing, or pharmacy at graduate level; financial need
$ Given: Five to nine grants; range, $500–$1,000
     Deadline: February 1

NEW JERSEY DEPARTMENT OF HIGHER EDUCATION

Edward J. Bloustein Distinguished Scholars Program
4 Quakerbridge Plaza, CN 540
Trenton, NJ 08625
(609) 588-3230; (800) 792-8670

Restrictions: New Jersey residents planning to enroll as full-time students at New Jersey colleges/universities, based on highest level of academic achievement (3.5 GPA); students may not apply directly to the program; candidates are selected for consideration by their secondary schools during their junior year.

$ Given: Grants average $1,000 per year, renewable for four years
Deadline: March 1

NEW JERSEY DEPARTMENT OF HIGHER EDUCATION

Educational Opportunity Fund Grant
4 Quakerbridge, Plaza, CD 540
Trenton, NJ 08625
(609) 588-3230; (800) 792-8670

Restrictions: Resident of New Jersey for at least 12 months who are full-time students in New Jersey college or institution and are economically and educationally disadvantaged with demonstrated financial need; must be matriculated; Garden State scholars can't apply for this grant.
$ Given: Varies, $400–$2,100 a year
   Deadlines: Determined by each school participating in the Educational Opportunity Fund

NEW JERSEY DEPARTMENT OF HIGHER EDUCATION

Garden State Scholarship Program
4 Quakerbridge, Plaza, CN 540
Trenton, NJ 08625
(609) 588-3230; (800) 792-8670

Contact: Leah Fletcher
Restrictions: Resident of New Jersey (minimum 12 months) to attend undergraduate student New Jersey institution; financial need; scholastic achievement based on high school records (3.5 GPA) and SAT scores; students must be nominated by their high schools by October 1 of their senior year.
$ Given: Unspecified number of $500 grants, renewable
   Deadline: October 1

NEW JERSEY DEPARTMENT OF HIGHER EDUCATION

Public Tuition Benefits Program
4 Quakerbridge, Plaza, CN 540
Trenton, NJ 08625
(609) 588-3230; (800) 792-8670

Contact: Leah Fletcher, Assistant Director,
Office of Grants and Scholarships
Restrictions: Spouses and children of New Jersey emergency personnel or law enforcement officers killed in the line of duty; New Jersey residents

attending New Jersey colleges/universities at least half-time as undergraduate students; renewable
$ Given: Full tuition at any New Jersey institution of higher education
 Deadlines: October 1 and March 1

NEW JERSEY DEPARTMENT OF HIGHER EDUCATION
Tuition Aid Grant (TAG)
4 Quakerbridge, Plaza, CN 540
Trenton, NJ 08625
(609) 588-3230

Contact: Leah Fletcher, Assistant Director, Office of Grants and Scholarships
Restrictions: Resident of New Jersey (minimum 12 months) to attend or
intend to attend New Jersey institutions; financial need; full-time undergraduate enrollment
$ Given: Unspecified number of $760–$5,570 grants; renewable
 Deadlines: June 1 for first-time applicants; October 1 for renewals

NEW YORK COUNCIL NAVY LEAGUE SCHOLARSHIP FUND
375 Park Avenue
Suite 3408
New York, NY 10152-1978
(212) 355-4960

Contact: Donald Sternberg, Executive Administrator
Restrictions: Must be dependent of an active or retired Navy, Marine
Corps, or Coast Guard service member; must be Connecticut, New Jersey,
or New York resident
$ Given: Approximately 13 $2,500 awards; renewable
 Deadline: June 15

NEW MEXICO

FFA WAL-MART SCHOLARSHIP
P.O. Box 15160
Alexandria, VA 22309-0160
(703) 360-3600

Restrictions: FFA member; freshman-year agriculture major; resident of Alabama, Arkansas, Arizona, California, Colorado, Connecticut, Delaware, Florida, Georgia, Hawaii, Idaho, Illinois, Indiana, Iowa, Kansas, Kentucky, Louisiana, Maine, Maryland, Michigan, Minnesota, Mississippi, Missouri, Montana, Nebraska, Nevada, New Hampshire, New Mexico, New York, North Carolina, North Dakota, Ohio, Oklahoma, Oregon, Pennsylvania, Puerto Rico, Rhode Island, South Carolina, South Dakota, Tennessee, Texas, Utah, Virginia, Washington State, West Virginia, Wisconsin, or Wyoming
$ Given: Approximately 50 awards of $1,000
Deadline: February 15

J. F. MADDOX FOUNDATION
Distinguished Scholarship Award
P.O. Box 2588
Hobbs, NM 88241-2588
(505) 393-6338

Contact: Robert Reid, Executive Director
Restrictions: Lee County residents; must have attended school in Lee County for minimum of two years
$ Loaned: Full scholarships
Deadline: June 30

NEW MEXICO MILITARY INSTITUTE
Eagle Scout Scholarship
101 West College
Roswell, NM 88201
(505) 622-6250

Restrictions: Members of Eagle Scout Association; single, male, under 23 years of age; agree to participate in NMMI scouting program
$ Given: One grant of $1,000
Deadline: April 1

NEW MEXICO VETERANS' SERVICE COMMISSION
Scholarship Program
P.O. Box 2324
Santa Fe, NM 87503
(505) 827-6300

Contact: Allen Martinez
Restrictions: Son or daughter (16 to 26) whose parent was killed in action, died, or was disabled as a result of military service in the U.S. armed forces during a time of armed conflict; undergraduate studies only
$ Given: 11 awards usually given
Deadline: None; applications may be submitted at any time

VILES FOUNDATION, INC.
c/o Nations Bank
P.O. Box 26900
Albuquerque, NM 87125-6900
(505) 765-2211

Restrictions: Residents of San Miguel and Mora counties, NM; financial need
$ Given: Unavailable
Deadline: April 1

NEW YORK

JESSIE H. BAKER EDUCATION FUND
c/o Marine Midland Bank
P.O. Box 719
Binghamton, NY 13902
(607) 772-5521

Contact: Kathleen Morris
Restrictions: Scholarships for undergraduate education for Broome County, NY, high school students; must include a SASE
$ Loaned: 25 loans of various amounts

BARUCH SCHOLARSHIPS
Baruch College of the City University of New York
Undergraduate Admission Office
P.O. Box 279
17 Lexington Avenue
New York, NY 10010

Contact: Ellen Washington, Admissions

Restrictions: Grants for Baruch College students
$ Given: Six grants averaging $2,600 each

THE JAMES GORDON BENNETT MEMORIAL CORPORATION

P.O. Box 307
East Rutherford, NJ 07073
(201) 438-1405

Restrictions: Children of persons who have worked at least 10 years for a New York City daily newspaper
$ Given: 70–80 grants, range, $500–$2,500
    Deadline: March 1

THE BUFFALO FOUNDATION

712 Main Street
Buffalo, NY 14202
(716) 852-2857

Contact: Gail Johnstone
Restrictions: Erie County, NY, residents; financial need
$ Given: 429 grants totaling $258,026 of various amounts
    Deadline: May 1

CHAUTAUQUA REGION COMMUNITY FOUNDATION, INC.

21 East Third Street, Suite 301
Jamestown, NY 14701
(716) 661-3390

Contact: Anna Carlson
Restrictions: Residents of Chautauqua County School District, Allegheny County
$ Given: 70 grants of various amounts awarded
    Deadlines: June 1, high school students; July 15, college students

CLARK FOUNDATION SCHOLARSHIP OFFICE

30 Wall Street, 9th Floor
New York, NY 10005
(212) 269-1833

Contact: Edward W. Stack, Secretary of Clark Foundation
Restrictions: Residents of 11 central districts in and around Cooper-

stown, NY; U.S. citizenship; upper 1/3 of class and 3.0 GPA
$ Given: 648 awards totaling $1,655,376; range, average: $2,000

BRUCE L. CRARY FOUNDATION, INC.
Hand House, River Street
P.O. Box 396
Elizabethtown, NY 12932
(518) 873-6496

Contact: Richard W. Lawrence, Jr., President
Restrictions: Residents of Clinton, Essex, Franklin, Hamilton, and Warren counties, NY
$ Given: 628 grants totaling $292,000
  Deadline: March 31

EDUCATIONAL OPPORTUNITY PROGRAM
New York State Higher Education Services Corporation
99 Washington Avenue
Albany, NY 12255
(518) 473-4563

Restrictions: New York State residents attending school in New York State; financial need
$ Given: Unavailable

FFA WAL-MART SCHOLARSHIP
P.O. Box 15160
Alexandria, VA 22309-0160
(703) 360-3600

Restrictions: FFA member; freshman-year agriculture major; resident of Alabama, Arkansas, Arizona, California, Colorado, Connecticut, Delaware, Florida, Georgia, Hawaii, Idaho, Illinois, Indiana, Iowa, Kansas, Kentucky, Louisiana, Maine, Maryland, Michigan, Minnesota, Mississippi, Missouri, Montana, Nebraska, Nevada, New Hampshire, New Mexico, New York, North Carolina, North Dakota, Ohio, Oklahoma, Oregon, Pennsylvania, Puerto Rico, Rhode Island, South Carolina, South Dakota, Tennessee, Texas, Utah, Virginia, Washington State, West Virginia, Wisconsin, or Wyoming

$ Given: Approximately 50 awards of $1,000
  Deadline: February 15

HIGHER EDUCATION OPPORTUNITY PROGRAM GRANT

99 Washington Avenue
Albany, NY 12255
(518) 473-4563

Restrictions: Economically and educationally disadvantaged New York residents attending New York schools
$ Given: Approximately 5,500 awards, range, $1,000–$2,000
  Deadlines: November 1, May 1

JEWISH FOUNDATION FOR EDUCATION OF WOMEN SCHOLARSHIP

330 West 58th Street
New York, NY 10019
(212) 265-2565

Contact: Florence Wallach, Executive Director
Restrictions: High school seniors who live within a 50-mile radius of New York City (including New Jersey and Long Island); law or M.B.A. candidates not eligible
$ Given: Annual awards, range, $500–$3,500
  Deadline: January 31

EDWIN T. MEREDITH FOUNDATION

Contact: Local County 4-H Office or State 4-H Office
Restrictions: Must be a 4-H member for at least one year; outstanding achievement; resident of Illinois, Indiana, Iowa, Kansas, Michigan, Minnesota, Missouri, Nebraska, New York, North Dakota, Ohio, Oklahoma, Pennsylvania, South Dakota, or Wisconsin
$ Given: Approximately three awards of $1,000
  Deadline: September 1

JAMES F. MULHOLLAND SCHOLARSHIP

112 State Street
Suite 400
Albany, NY 12207
(518) 463-2215

Contact: Richard Pedro
Restrictions: New York State resident who is a child of a New York legionnaire.

$ Given: Awards up to $500
   Deadline: May 1

NEW YORK AID FOR PART-TIME STUDY

New York State Higher Education Services Corporation
99 Washington Avenue
Albany, NY 12255
(518) 473-4563

Restrictions: New York State residents enrolled part-time at
New York schools
$ Given: Awards up to $2,000 per student

NEW YORK COUNCIL NAVY LEAGUE SCHOLARSHIP

375 Park Avenue
Suite 3408
New York, NY 10152
(212) 355-4960

Contact: Donald Sternberg
Restrictions: Must be dependent of an active or reserve Navy, Marine
Corps, or Coast Guard service member; must be Connecticut, New Jersey,
or New York resident
$ Given: Approximately five $2,500 awards
   Deadline: June 15

NEW YORK STATE HIGHER EDUCATION
SERVICES CORPORATION

Robert C. Byrd Honors Scholarship
Cultural Education Center-SASS
Albany, NY 12230
(518) 486-1319

Contact: New York State Department of Education, Bureau of Elementary and Secondary Testing, (518) 474-8684
Restrictions: New York residents, based on SAT or ACT scores and high
school achievement; age: 20 or under
$ Given: 400 awards for $1,500 each
   Deadline: March 1

NEW YORK STATE HIGHER EDUCATION SERVICES CORPORATION

Guaranteed Student Loan Program
Student Information
Cultural Education Center-SASS
Albany, NY 12230
(518) 473-8567

Restrictions: Resident of New York enrolled at least half time at an approved postsecondary institution (U.S. and foreign); U.S. citizens and legal residents
$ Loaned: Unspecified number of loans up to $2,625; renewable
  Deadline: March 31

NEW YORK STATE HIGHER EDUCATION SERVICES CORPORATION

Regents Grants for Children of Deceased or Disabled Veterans
Student Information
Cultural Education Center-SASS
Albany, NY 12230
(518) 473-1574

Restrictions: Residents of New York; children of disabled, deceased MIA or POW veterans who served in the U.S. armed forces during certain specified periods; for undergraduate study or vocational/technical training
$ Given: Unspecified number of $450 grants; renewable for four years
  Deadline: May 1

NEW YORK STATE HIGHER EDUCATION SERVICES CORPORATION

Regents Grants for Children of Deceased Police Officers and Firefighters
Student Information
Cultural Education Center-SASS
Albany, NY 12230
(518) 473-1574

Restrictions: Resident of New York; children of New York resident police officers, firefighters (including volunteer firefighters) or corrections officers who died as the result of injuries sustained in the line of duty; for undergraduate study or vocational/technical training in New York State
$ Given: Unspecified number of $450 grants; renewable for four years
  Deadline: May 1

NEW YORK STATE HIGHER EDUCATION SERVICES CORPORATION

Tuition Assistance Program (TAP Grants)
Student Information
Cultural Education Center-SASS
Albany, NY 12230
(518) 474-5642

Restrictions: New York residents enrolled full time in an approved two-to-four year New York institution; U.S. citizens and legal residents; financial need required
$ Given: Unspecified number of grants of $375–$3,900 ($100–$1,200 for graduate students); renewable through doctoral program
  Deadline: May 1

NEW YORK STATE HIGHER EDUCATION SERVICES CORPORATION

Vietnam Veterans Tuition Grants
Student Information
Cultural Education Center-SASS
Albany, NY 12230
(518) 473-1574

Restrictions: Residents of New York; Vietnam veterans enrolled at an approved New York institution (for undergraduate study or vocational/technical training)
$ Given: Unspecified number of grants of $250–$500 per semester; renewable up to four years
  Deadline: May 1

NORTHERN NEW YORK COMMUNITY FOUNDATION

120 Washington Street
Watertown, NY 13601
(315) 782-7110

Contact: Alex Vetto, Executive Director
Restrictions: Residents of Lewis and Jefferson counties, NY; undergraduates enrolled in accredited continental U.S. colleges and universities; demonstrate academic achievement and financial need
$ Given: Grants totaling $200,000; range, $100–$5,000
  Deadline: April 1

OPPENHEIM STUDENTS FUND, INC.

Barbara Joyce, Board of Education
607 Walnut Avenue
Niagara Falls, NY 14303
(716) 286-4220

Restrictions: High school seniors who are current residents of Niagara County, NY
$ Given: General range, $250–$2,000
    Deadline: April 1

ROCHESTER INSTITUTE OF TECHNOLOGY

Urban League Minority Scholarships
Financial Aid Office
Rochester Institute of Technology, Bausch and Lomb Center
1 Lomb Memorial Drive
Rochester, NY 14623-5604
(716) 475-2186

Contact: Verna Haven
Restrictions: Minority students attending R.I.T.
$ Given: 40 awards of varying amounts

ROOTHBERT FUND, INC.

475 Riverside Drive, Room 252
New York, NY 10115
(212) 870-3116

Contact: Jacob Van Rossum, Administrative Secretary
Restrictions: Preference given to persons motivated by spiritual values who are considering teaching as their vocation; must appear in New York for interview
$ Given: Grants totaling $59,000; range, $1,500–$2,000, renewable
    Deadline: February 1; applications available after December 1; send SASE for prompt response

SCALP AND BLADE SCHOLARSHIP TRUST

Scalp and Blade, Inc.
164 Cayuga Road
Buffalo, NY 14225-1910

Contact:　Walter N. Cunz, Chairman Scholarship Committee
Restrictions:　Male high school seniors from Erie County, NY, who plan
to attend schools outside Erie and Niagara counties
$ Given:　four awards of $750
　　Deadline:　May 31

THE LEOPOLD SCHEPP FOUNDATION

551 Fifth Avenue, Suite 3000
New York, NY 10176-2597
(212) 986-3078

Contact:　Mrs. Edythe Bobrow, Executive Secretary
Restrictions:　U.S. citizens; undergraduates under 30 years of age; GPA
4.0; financial need; send SASE
$ Given:　150 to 200 grants; range, $1,000–$7,500
　　Deadline:　November 1

THOMAS C. SHARPE MEMORIAL SCHOLARSHIP

Department of Planning and Community Development
9 South First Avenue
Ninth Floor
Mount Vernon, NY 10550
(914) 699-7230

Contact:　Donna Fulco, Scholarship Program Manager
Restrictions:　Residents of Mount Vernon, NY, with minimum 2.0 GPA;
financial need
$ Given:　122 grants; range, $300–$800
　　Deadline:　First Friday in June

SKIDMORE COLLEGE

Filene Music Scholarships
Skidmore College
Saratoga Springs, NY 12866
(518) 584-5000

Contact:　Robert Shorb, Director of Financial Aid
Restrictions:　Scholarships to worthy music students of Skidmore
$ Given:　four grants totaling $24,000

STATE AID TO NATIVE AMERICANS
New York State Higher Education Services Corporation
99 Washington Avenue
Albany, NY 12255
(518) 474-0537

Contacts: NY State Education Dept.; Native American Education Unit
Restrictions: New York residents on official tribal rolls of New York State tribes (or children of such members) who are enrolled in approved postsecondary programs in New York; academic achievement
$ Given: All eligible applicants receive funding; range, $456–$1,500
    Deadlines: August 1, December 31, and May 20

STONY-WOLD HERBERT FUND, INC.
136 East 57th Street, Room 1705
New York, NY 10022
(212) 753-6565

Contact: Ms. Cheryl S. Friedman, Executive Director
Restrictions: New York City metropolitan area students with respiratory illnesses
$ Given: 30 grants totaling $60,000

UNITED FEDERATION OF TEACHERS
College Scholarship Fund
260 Park Avenue South
Sixth Floor
New York, NY 10010
(212) 529-2110 Fax (212) 533-2704

Contact: Harriet Merchant, Director of Scholarships
Restrictions: New York resident; age 20 or under; intend to pursue undergraduate studies; financial need
$ Given: 250 awards for $1,000 each; renewable up to four years.
    Deadline: December 3

DAVID WASSERMAN SCHOLARSHIP FUND, INC.
4722 State Highway 30
Amsterdam, NY 12010
(518) 843-2800

Contact: Norbert J. Sherbunt, President
Restrictions: Montgomery County, NY, residents
$ Given: Unavailable
    Deadline: June 30

NORTH CAROLINA

ROBERT C. BYRD HONORS SCHOLARSHIP
301 North Wilmington Street
Raleigh, NC, 27601-2825
(919) 715-1120

Restrictions: North Carolina resident who graduated from a North Carolina school; academic merit
$ Given: $1,500

FFA WAL-MART SCHOLARSHIP
P.O. Box 15160
Alexandria, VA 22309-0160
(703) 360-3600

Restrictions: FFA member; freshman-year agriculture major; resident of Alabama, Arkansas, Arizona, California, Colorado, Connecticut, Delaware, Florida, Georgia, Hawaii, Idaho, Illinois, Indiana, Iowa, Kansas, Kentucky, Louisiana, Maine, Maryland, Michigan, Minnesota, Mississippi, Missouri, Montana, Nebraska, Nevada, New Hampshire, New Mexico, New York, North Carolina, North Dakota, Ohio, Oklahoma, Oregon, Pennsylvania, Puerto Rico, Rhode Island, South Carolina, South Dakota, Tennessee, Texas, Utah, Virginia, Washington State, West Virginia, Wisconsin, or Wyoming
$ Given: Approximately 50 awards of $1,000
    Deadline: February 15

FOUNDATION FOR THE CAROLINAS
1043 East Morehead Street, Suite 100
Charlotte, NC 28204

Contact: William Spencer, President

Restrictions: Given to students in North Carolina and South Carolina
$ Given: 300 grants of various amounts

JAMES LEE LOVE SCHOLARSHIPS

North Carolina State Education
Assistance Authority
P.O. Box 2688
Chapel Hill, NC 27515-2688

Contacts: UNC financial aid office
Restrictions: Full-time North Carolina residents attending one of the campuses of the University of North Carolina; financial need
$ Given: $3,500

NORTH CAROLINA ASSOCIATION OF INSURANCE AGENTS SCHOLARSHIP

1506 Hillsborough Street
P.O. Box 10097
Raleigh, NC 27605
(919) 828-4371

Contact: Jeanne Hess Clin
Restrictions: North Carolina resident; academic merit: financial need; must be sponsored by an independent insurance agent who belongs to the Big I association
$ Given: Approximately 60 $1,000 awards
  Deadline: April 1

NORTH CAROLINA DIVISION OF VETERANS AFFAIRS

Scholarship Program
325 North Salisbury Street, Albemarle Building
Suite, 1065
Raleigh, NC 27603
(919) 733-3851

Contact: Charles F. Smith
Restrictions: Sons and daughters of veterans who died or were disabled as a result of wartime service; also POWs, MIAs; either the parent must have entered the armed forces as a North Carolina resident, or the applicant must have been born in North Carolina and lived there since birth and attended school in North Carolina.

$ Given: Approximately 400 awards, range, $1,500–$4,500
   Deadline: May 31

NORTH CAROLINA FRESHMEN SCHOLARS PROGRAM
University of North Carolina, General Administration
P.O. Box 2688
Chapel Hill NC, 27515-2688

Restrictions: High school seniors, North Carolina residents planning to attend a North Carolina school
$ Given: Freshman year tuition, fees, and books

NORTH CAROLINA STATE ASSISTANCE AUTHORITY
Minority Presence Grant
Scholarship and Grant Services
North Carolina State Education Assistance Authority
P.O. Box 2688
Chapel Hill, NC 27515-2688

Restrictions: North Carolina resident attending North Carolina school where grant recipient is member of an ethnic group that is in the minority at the school; financial need
$ Given: Varying amounts depending on the financial need of each recipient and availability of funds

NORTH CAROLINA TEACHING FELLOWS PROGRAM
North Carolina Teaching Fellows Commission
Roger Center, Cumberland Building
3739 National Drive, Suite 210
Raleigh, NC 27612

Restrictions: North Carolina high school graduates entering teacher-training programs; must teach in North Carolina public school for four years or repay award
$ Given: Up to $5,000 per year

NUCOR FOUNDATION, INC.
2100 Rexford Road
Charlotte, NC 28211
(704) 366-7000

Contact: Elizabeth Wells
Restrictions: Children of Nucor, Inc., employees only; must maintain 2.0 GPA in college
$ Given: Up to $2,000 per year for four years
   Deadline: March 1

SPRINT/CAROLINA TELEPHONE SCHOLARSHIP PROGRAM

North Carolina Department
of Community Colleges
3344 Caswell Building
200 West Jones Street
Raleigh, NC 27603-1337

Contact: Financial aid office of community college attended
Restrictions: North Carolina residents enrolled at North Carolina community colleges; minimum 2.5 GPA; financial need
$ Given: 20 awards of $500

STONECUTTER FOUNDATION, INC.

Dallas Street
Spindale, NC 28160
(704) 286-2341

Contact: Van Lonon, Treasurer
Restrictions: Residents of Rutherford and Polk counties, NC
$ Loaned: 25 loans totaling $21,150; range, $500–$2,000

THE WINSTON-SALEM FOUNDATION

860 W. 5th Street
Winston-Salem, NC 27101-2506
(336) 725-2832

Contact: K. Dylan, Assistant Director of Student Aid
Restrictions: Residents of Forsythe County, NC
$ Given: Unspecified number of grants and loans; maximum award $2,500; $10,000 total over four years
   Deadline: None

NORTH DAKOTA

AMERICAN LEGION, NATIONAL HIGH SCHOOL
Oratorical Contest
American Legion, Department of North Dakota
1626 North 26th Street
Bismarck, ND 58501-3035

Contact: Mr. Vern Fetch
Restrictions: North Dakota high school student age 16–19; oratorical contest; must speak on the topic of the U.S. Constitution
$ Given: Approximately 38 awards, range, $100–$1,900
   Deadline: January 31

GABRIEL J. BROWN TRUST
112 Avenue East West
Bismarck, ND 58501
(701) 223-5916

Contact: Susan Lundberg
Restrictions: Residents of North Dakota
$ Loaned: Unavailable
   Deadline: June 15

PAUL DOUGLAS TEACHER SCHOLARSHIP
600 East Boulevard
Bismarck, ND 58505-0230

Restrictions: North Dakota resident pursuing a degree in education; top 10% of class
$ Given: Awards up to $5,000
   Deadline: April 15

FFA WAL-MART SCHOLARSHIP
P.O. Box 15160
Alexandria, VA 22309-0160
(703) 360-3600

Restrictions: FFA member; freshman-year agriculture major; resident of Alabama, Arkansas, Arizona, California, Colorado, Connecticut, Delaware, Florida, Georgia, Hawaii, Idaho, Illinois, Indiana, Iowa, Kansas,

Kentucky, Louisiana, Maine, Maryland, Michigan, Minnesota, Mississippi, Missouri, Montana, Nebraska, Nevada, New Hampshire, New Mexico, New York, North Carolina, North Dakota, Ohio, Oklahoma, Oregon, Pennsylvania, Puerto Rico, Rhode Island, South Carolina, South Dakota, Tennessee, Texas, Utah, Virginia, Washington State, West Virginia, Wisconsin, or Wyoming
$ Given: Approximately 50 awards of $1,000
  Deadline: February 15

EDWIN T. MEREDITH FOUNDATION

Contact: Local County 4-H Office or State 4-H Office
Restrictions: Must be a 4-H member for at least one year; outstanding achievement; resident of Illinois, Indiana, Iowa, Kansas, Michigan, Minnesota, Missouri, Nebraska, New York, North Dakota, Ohio, Oklahoma, Pennsylvania, South Dakota, or Wisconsin
$ Given: Approximately three awards of $1,000
  Deadline: September 1

NORTH DAKOTA INDIAN SCHOLARSHIP PROGRAM

State Capitol Building
600 East Boulevard, 10th Floor
Bismarck, ND 58505-0230
(701) 328-2166

Restrictions: Residents of North Dakota; at least 1/4 Indian blood and an enrolled member of a tribe now North Dakota resident; high school diploma or GED certificate; financial need
$ Given: 70–100 scholarships up to $2,000 per year, renewable
  Deadline: July 15

NORTH DAKOTA SCHOLARS PROGRAM

c/o Student Financial Assistance Program
North Dakota University System
State Capitol, Building
600 East Boulevard, 10th Floor
Bismarck, ND 58505-0230

Restrictions: High school seniors who score at or above 95% on ACT assessment and rank in top 20% of class; attend state school
$ Given: Full tuition

NORTH DAKOTA STATE GRANT PROGRAM
State Capitol Building
600 East Boulevard, 10th Floor
Bismarck, ND 58505-0230
(701) 328-2960

Contact: Peggy Wipf
Restrictions: North Dakota residents planning to attend college in North Dakota; rank in top 20% of graduating class and score in top 5% of ACT assessment; renewable
$ Given: 50 awards, range, $1,150–$1,500

NORTH DAKOTA STUDENT FINANCIAL ASSISTANCE GRANTS
Student Financial Assistance Program
North Dakota University System
Capitol Building, 10th Floor
600 East Boulevard
Bismarck, ND 58505-0230

Restrictions: Residents of North Dakota for study at North Dakota institutions; financial need
$ Given: Grants of up to $600; renewable
   Deadline: April 15

TREACY COMPANY
Box 1700
Helena, MT 59624-1700
(406) 442-3632

Contact: James O'Connell
Restrictions: Residents of, or freshman or sophomore year students attending institutions in Idaho, Montana, North Dakota, and South Dakota
$ Given: 80 grants totaling $22,500; average grant, $500
   Deadline: June 15

HIO

AVON PRODUCTS, INC.
Avon Scholarship Program
175 Progress Place

Cincinnati, OH 45246
(513) 551-2752

Contact: Kristen Ziegler
Restrictions: Residents of Ohio; graduating high school seniors from Princeton, Ramapo, Morton Grove, and Pasadena school districts who are in the top 10% of their class; U.S. citizens or legal residents and whose parents are employees of Avon
$ Given: Unspecified number of $3,000 grants, renewable
   Deadline: November 1

DEPARTMENT PRESIDENT'S SCHOLARSHIP

1100 Brandywine Blvd, Building D
P.O. Box 2279
Zanesville, OH 43702-2279
(614) 452-8245

Contact: Doris Wainwright
Restrictions: Child or grandchild of a living or deceased veteran; Ohio resident; must be sponsored by an American Legion Auxiliary unit; freshman year
$ Given: Award range $1,000–$1,500
   Deadline: March 15

FFA WAL-MART SCHOLARSHIP

P.O. Box 15160
Alexandria, VA 22309-0160
(703) 360-3600

Restrictions: FFA member; freshman-year agriculture major; resident of Alabama, Arkansas, Arizona, California, Colorado, Connecticut, Delaware, Florida, Georgia, Hawaii, Idaho, Illinois, Indiana, Iowa, Kansas, Kentucky, Louisiana, Maine, Maryland, Michigan, Minnesota, Mississippi, Missouri, Montana, Nebraska, Nevada, New Hampshire, New Mexico, New York, North Carolina, North Dakota, Ohio, Oklahoma, Oregon, Pennsylvania, Puerto Rico, Rhode Island, South Carolina, South Dakota, Tennessee, Texas, Utah, Virginia, Washington State, West Virginia, Wisconsin, or Wyoming
$ Given: Approximately 50 awards of $1,000
   Deadline: February 15

THE S.N. FORD AND ADA FORD FUND
c/o Key Trust Company of Ohio, N.A.
P.O. Box 849
Mansfield, OH 44901
(419) 525-7671

Contact: Nick Gesouras
Restrictions: Residents of Richland County, OH
$ Given: Average grant $400–$450

HAUSS-HELMS FOUNDATION, INC.
Fifth 3rd Bank
P.O. Box 25
Wapakoneta, OH 45895
(419) 738-4911

Contact: James E. Weger, President
Restrictions: Graduating seniors of Auglaize and Allen counties, OH;
financial need; have at least 2.0 GPA
$ Given: 600 grants; range, $400–$5,000
  Deadline: April 15

BLANCHE AND THOMAS HOPE FUND
c/o National City Bank
P.O. Box 1270
Ashland, KY 41101
(606) 329-2900

Restrictions: Graduating seniors from Boyd and Greenup counties, KY,
and Lawrence County, OH
$ Given: 100 grants totaling $120,000; range, $90–$2,500
  Deadline: March 1

KENT STATE UNIVERSITY
Oscar Ritchie Memorial Scholarship
P.O. Box 5190
Kent, OH 44242-0001
(216) 672-2972

Contact: Connie Dubick, Financial Officer

Restrictions: Minority students with financial needs; good academic standing
$ Given: 118 grants of various amounts awarded

EDWIN L. AND LOUIS B. MCCALLAY EDUCATIONAL TRUST FUND

c/o Norman N. Hayes, Ed.D. of Southwestern Ohio, Trust Division
Middletown Center Foundation
29 City Center Plaza
Middletown, OH 45042
(513) 424-7369

Contact: Norman M. Hayes, Director
Restrictions: Middletown, OH, city school district graduates
$ Given: Grant range, $100–$800
   Deadline: February 28

JOHN MCINTIRE EDUCATIONAL FUND

c/o First Financial Services, Trust Department
P.O. Box 2458
Zanesville, OH 43702
(740) 452-8444

Contact: Nina Butler, Senior Trust Officer
Restrictions: Unmarried students under 21 years of age who live within the city limits of Zanesville, OH
$ Given: 140 grants totaling $144,075; range, $250–$1,600
   Deadline: May 1

EDWIN T. MEREDITH FOUNDATION

Contact: Local County 4-H Office or State 4-H Office
Restrictions: Must be a 4-H member for at least one year; outstanding achievement; resident of Illinois, Indiana, Iowa, Kansas, Michigan, Minnesota, Missouri, Nebraska, New York, North Dakota, Ohio, Oklahoma, Pennsylvania, South Dakota, or Wisconsin
$ Given: Approximately three awards of $1,000
   Deadline: September 1

NEW ORPHAN ASYLUM SCHOLARSHIP FOUNDATION
2340 Victory Parkway, Suite One
Cincinnati, OH 45206
(513) 961-6626

Contact: Melody Dunn Sparks, Administrator
Restrictions: Residents of the greater Cincinnati, OH, area
$ Given: 89 grants totaling $89,000; each for $1,000
  Deadline: July 31

OHIO STUDENT AID COMMISSION
Ohio Academic Scholarship Plan
P.O. Box 182452
Columbus, OH 43218-2452
(614) 466-8716

Restrictions: Residents of Ohio; seniors at eligible Ohio high schools; outstanding academic performance; to attend eligible Ohio institutions of higher education full time; U.S. citizens
$ Given: 1,000 grants of $2,000; automatically renewable up to four years with satisfactory academic progress
  Deadline: October 1

OHIO STUDENT AID COMMISSION
Ohio Instructional Grants
P.O. Box 182452
Columbus, OH 43218-2452
(614) 466-8716

Restrictions: Residents of Ohio enrolled full time in eligible Ohio or Pennsylvania institutions of nursing; good academic standing; financial need; U.S. citizens
$ Given: 270,000 grants totaling $6 million; average grant: $630
  Deadline: October 1

OHIO STUDENT AID COMMISSION
Ohio Student Choice Grant
P.O. Box 182452
Columbus, OH 43218-2452
(614) 466-8716

Restrictions: Residents of Ohio enrolled full time in an eligible private

nonprofit college or university; not for study leading to degrees in religion or theology; U.S. citizens
$ Given: 23,000 grants up to $678; renewable to five years
Deadlines: Determined by institutions, Ohio Board of Regents

OHIO STUDENT LOAN COMMISSION
Robert C. Byrd Honors Scholarship
P.O. Box 16610
Columbus, OH 43216-6610
(614) 644-8892 and (800) 837-6752

Contact: Ohio Student Aid Commission, Customer Service Department
Restrictions: Ohio residents demonstrating exceptional academic achievement
$ Given: 270 awards for $1,500 each
Deadline: March 10

OHIO WAR ORPHANS SCHOLARSHIP BOARD
P.O. Box 182452
Columbus, OH 43218-2452
(614) 466-8716

Restrictions: Dependents of Ohio veterans killed in action or who served at least 90 days in wartime resulting in 60% disability; or 100% disability for any reason; minimum of 2.0 GPA required; age: from 16 to 21
$ Given: 350 grants, full tuition at public school or equivalent amount at private schools; automatic renewal for up to four years
Deadline: July 1

PART-TIME STUDENT INSTRUCTIONAL GRANT PROGRAM
P.O. Box 16610
Columbus, OH 43216-6610
(614) 644-8892
Restrictions: Ohio resident attending Ohio school part-time; special consideration given to single heads of households or displaced homemakers
$ Given: Grant range, $250–$3,000

THE RATNER, MILLER, SHAFRAN FOUNDATION
50 Public Square # 1100
Cleveland, OH 44113
(216) 621-6060

Restrictions: Students attending college in the U.S.; must reside in Ohio
$ Given: Average award $500
    Deadline: May 1

GEORGE J. RECORD
SCHOOL FOUNDATION
365 Main Street
Conneaut, OH 44030
(216) 599-8283

Contact: Charles N. Lafferty, President and Executive Director
Restrictions: Residents of Ashtabula County, OH; must attend approved private college and complete six quarter hours of religious study (Protestant); financial need
$ Given: 64 to 82 grants; range, $500–$3,000

THE RICHLAND COUNTY FOUNDATION
OF MANSFIELD, OHIO
24 West 3rd Street
Suite 100
Mansfield, OH 44902
(419) 525-3020

Contact: Pam Siegenthaler, President
Restrictions: Residents of Richland County, OH; full-time undergraduate students; financial need
$ Given: Grants totaling approximately $150,000
    Deadline: May 1

SCHOLARSHIP FUND, INC.
c/o Dean Ernest Weaver, Jr., Secretary
University of Toledo
2801 West Bancroft Street
Toledo, OH 43606-3390
(419) 530-3133

Restrictions: Residents of the northwest Ohio area; preference given to undergraduate upper division who are commuting; financial need; high scholastic ranking
$ Given: 24 grants totaling $24,033; range, $400–$1,600

THE VAN WERT COUNTY FOUNDATION
138 East Main Street
Van Wert, OH 45891
(419) 238-1743

Contact: Larry L. Wendel, Executive Secretary
Restrictions: Van Wert County and Pauling County, OH, residents;
scholarships in art, music, agriculture, and home economics
$ Given: 170 grants totaling $216,000; range, $400–$3,000
   Deadline: June 1

OKLAHOMA

ACADEMIC SCHOLARS PROGRAM
Oklahoma State Regents for Higher Education
500 Education Building
Oklahoma City, OK 73105

Restrictions: Attend Oklahoma school; must have graduated from high
school after July 1, 1988, high academic achievement; have an ACT score
at or above the 99.5 percentile
$ Given: Awards range, $3,000–$5,000

CHEROKEE NATION OF OKLAHOMA
P.O. Box 948
Tahlequah, OK 74465
(918) 456-0671 or (800) 722-4325

Contact: Grant Administrator
Restrictions: One-quarter or more Cherokee Indian to attend college or
university in U.S.; financial need; U.S. citizens only
$ Given: 500 grants annually; range, $750–$1,500
   Deadline: April 1

CHEYENNE-ARAPAHO TRIBAL SCHOLARSHIP
P.O. Box 38
Concho, OK 73022
(405) 262-0345

Contact: Teresa Dorsett
Restrictions: Oklahoma resident who is a member of the Cheyenne-Arapaho tribe; minimum 2.0 GPA; financial need
$ Given: Approximately 100 awards, range, $100–$2,000
   Deadlines: June 1 (fall), November 1 (spring)

FFA WAL-MART SCHOLARSHIP
P.O. Box 15160
Alexandria, VA 22309-0160
(703) 360-3600

Restrictions: FFA member; freshman-year agriculture major; resident of Alabama, Arkansas, Arizona, California, Colorado, Connecticut, Delaware, Florida, Georgia, Hawaii, Idaho, Illinois, Indiana, Iowa, Kansas, Kentucky, Louisiana, Maine, Maryland, Michigan, Minnesota, Mississippi, Missouri, Montana, Nebraska, Nevada, New Hampshire, New Mexico, New York, North Carolina, North Dakota, Ohio, Oklahoma, Oregon, Pennsylvania, Puerto Rico, Rhode Island, South Carolina, South Dakota, Tennessee, Texas, Utah, Virginia, Washington State, West Virginia, Wisconsin, or Wyoming
$ Given: Approximately 50 awards of $1,000
   Deadline: February 15

LAURA FIELDS TRUST
P.O. Box 2394
Lawton, OK 73502
(580) 355-3733

Contact: Jay Dee Fountain, Executive Secretary
Restrictions: Residents of Southwest Oklahoma in college
and graduate school
$ Loaned: Loans totaling $60,000; average: $2,000 per year,
renewable

EDWIN T. MEREDITH FOUNDATION

Contact: Local County 4-H Office or State 4-H Office
Restrictions: Must be a 4-H member for at least one year; outstanding achievement; resident of Illinois, Indiana, Iowa, Kansas, Michigan, Minnesota, Missouri, Nebraska, New York, North Dakota, Ohio, Oklahoma,

Pennsylvania, South Dakota, or Wisconsin
$ Given: Approximately three awards of $1,000
    Deadline: September 1

OKLAHOMA TUITION AID GRANT

Tuition Aid Grant Program
Oklahoma State Regents for Higher Education
P.O. Box 3020
Oklahoma City, OK 73101-3020

Contact: High school guidance office or college financial aid office
Restrictions: Oklahoma residents to attend Oklahoma schools;
financial need
$ Given: Awards up to $1,000; renewable
    Deadline: April 30

WILLIAM P. WILLIS SCHOLARSHIP

500 Education Building
State Capitol Complex
Oklahoma City, OK 73105
(405) 524-9153

Contact: Dawn Scott
Restrictions: Oklahoma resident; financial need
$ Given: One award per school, range, $1,500–$2,400
    Deadline: Late May

OREGON

ACHIEVEMENT AWARDS

1242 University of Oregon
Eugene, OR 97403-1242
(503) 346-3044

Contact: James Gilmour, Associate Director of Financial Aid
Restrictions: Academic merit and financial need
$ Given: Unspecified number; range, $1,200–$2,700
    Deadline: February 1

ROBERT C. BYRD HONORS SCHOLARSHIP
Oregon State Scholarship Commission
1500 Valley River Drive, Suite 100
Eugene, OR 97401-7020

Contact: Mr. James Beyer
Restrictions: Oregon high school seniors with a minimum GPA of 3.85 and combined SAT scores of at least 1150 or ACT scores of at least 27
$ Given: Approximately 75 awards of $1,500; renewable
Deadline: March 1

COLLINS-MCDONALD TRUST FUND
P.O. Box 351
Lakeview, OR 97630
(503) 947-2196

Contact: James C. Lynch, Trustee
Restrictions: Residents and graduates of Lake County, OR, high schools
$ Given: 25 grants totaling $38,940; range, $610–$2,520
Deadline: May 1

BERNARD DANY EDUCATIONAL FUND
620 North First Street
P.O. Box 351
Lakeview, OR 97630
(503) 947-2196

Contact: James C. Lynch
Restrictions: Graduates of Lake County, OR, high school
$ Given: 60 grants; average: $2,100
Deadline: May 1

FFA WAL-MART SCHOLARSHIP
P.O. Box 15160
Alexandria, VA 22309-0160
(703) 360-3600

Restrictions: FFA member; freshman-year agriculture major; resident of Alabama, Arkansas, Arizona, California, Colorado, Connecticut, Delaware, Florida, Georgia, Hawaii, Idaho, Illinois, Indiana, Iowa, Kansas, Kentucky, Louisiana, Maine, Maryland, Michigan, Minnesota, Mississippi, Missouri, Montana, Nebraska, Nevada, New Hampshire, New Mexico,

New York, North Carolina, North Dakota, Ohio, Oklahoma, Oregon, Pennsylvania, Puerto Rico, Rhode Island, South Carolina, South Dakota, Tennessee, Texas, Utah, Virginia, Washington State, West Virginia, Wisconsin, or Wyoming
$ Given: Approximately 50 awards of $1,000
  Deadline: February 15

FORD FAMILY FOUNDATION SCHOLARSHIP
1500 Valley River Drive, Suite 100
Eugene, OR 97401
(541) 687-7395

Contact: Jim Beyer
Restrictions: Oregon resident attending Oregon school; minimum 3.0 GPA; financial need
$ Given: $1,000–$10,000
  Deadline: March 1

OREGON AFL-CIO ASAT-MAY DARLING SCHOLARSHIP
Oregon AFL CIO
1900 Hines Street SE
Salem, OR 97302
(503) 585-6320

Contact: Amy Klare, Research and Education Director
Restrictions: Oregon residents graduating from accredited Oregon high schools; based on written essay, financial need, high school GPA, and interview; intend to attend a certified trade school
$ Given: 6 awards maximum; $600, $1,000, and $3,000
  Deadline: February 15

OREGON DEPARTMENT OF VETERANS' AFFAIRS
Educational Scholarship Aid for Oregon Veterans
700 Summer Street N.E., Suite 150
Salem, OR 97310
(503) 373-2085

Restrictions: Resident of Oregon at time of application; for study in accredited Oregon institution; must have qualifying military service record; U.S. citizen
$ Given: Grants of approximately $50 per month to each eligible veteran
  Deadline: None

OREGON NEED GRANT
1500 Valley River Drive, Suite 100
Eugene, OR 97401
(541) 687-7395

Contact: Jim Beyer
Restrictions: Oregon resident attending Oregon school full-time;
financial need
$ Given: Approximately 24,000 awards, range, $850–$1,500
   Deadline: Varies

OREGON PTA
Teacher Education Scholarships
531 Southeast 14th Street
Portland, OR 97214
(503) 234-3928

Restrictions: Oregon residents planning to each in Oregon at the elementary and secondary level; to attend any public Oregon college or university
$ Given: Unspecified number of $500 grants
   Deadline: March 1

PACIFIC PRINTING AND IMAGING ASSOCIATION
Educational Trust Scholarships
180 Nickerson, Suite 102
Seattle, WA 98109

Contact: Jim Olsen
Restrictions: Students studying printing, print management, or graphic
arts technology; must live in Washington, Oregon, Arkansas, Idaho, Montana, or Hawaii
$ Given: 12 awards, range, $500–$2,500; renewable
   Deadline: April 1

JACK SHININ MEMORIAL SCHOLARSHIP
1500 Valley River Drive, Suite 100
Eugene, OR 97401
(503) 687-7395

Contact: Jim Beyer
Restrictions: Afro-American, Hispanic, or Native American Oregon resi-

dents attending Oregon schools; financial need; freshman year
$ Given: Average award $1,000
    Deadline: March 1

JEROME B. STEINBACH SCHOLARSHIP

Oregon State Scholarship Commission
1500 Valley River Drive, Suite 100
Eugene, OR 97401-7020

Contact: Mr. James Beyer or college financial aid office
Restrictions: Oregon residents attending Oregon schools; sophomores, juniors, or seniors; minimum 3.25 GPA
$ Given: Approximately 50 awards, range, $500–$1,000
    Deadline: March 1

WESTON FAMILY SCHOLARSHIP

1500 Valley River Drive, Suite 100
Eugene, OR 97401
(503) 687-7395

Contact: Jim Beyer
Restrictions: Oregon resident; graduate of Astoria, Benson, Central Catholic, Cleveland, Franklin, Grant, Jefferson, La Salle, Lincoln, Madison, Marshall, Roosevelt, St. Mary's Academy, or Wilson high schools; attend Oregon school; financial need
$ Given: $1,000
    Deadline: March 1

MARIA C. JACKSON–GENERAL GEORGE A. WHITE STUDENT AID FUND

c/o U.S. Bank of Oregon, Trust Group
1500 Valley River Drive, Suite 100
Eugene, OR 97401
(541) 687-7395

Restrictions: U.S. armed forces veterans or children of veterans who are longtime Oregon residents to study in Oregon; have at least 3.75 GPA; financial need
$ Given: Amounts vary
    Deadline: March 1

PENNSYLVANIA

AMERICAN LEGION ORATORICAL CONTEST
American Legion, Department of Pennsylvania
P.O. Box 2324
Harrisburg, PA 17105-2324

Contact: Rebecca A. Susaridge
Restrictions: High school student age 20 or under; Pennsylvania resident; public speaking
$ Given: Three awards, range, $1,000–$2,000
   Deadline: February 1

FFA WAL-MART SCHOLARSHIP
P.O. Box 15160
Alexandria, VA 22309-0160
(703) 360-3600

Restrictions: FFA member; freshman-year agriculture major; resident of Alabama, Arkansas, Arizona, California, Colorado, Connecticut, Delaware, Florida, Georgia, Hawaii, Idaho, Illinois, Indiana, Iowa, Kansas, Kentucky, Louisiana, Maine, Maryland, Michigan, Minnesota, Mississippi, Missouri, Montana, Nebraska, Nevada, New Hampshire, New Mexico, New York, North Carolina, North Dakota, Ohio, Oklahoma, Oregon, Pennsylvania, Puerto Rico, Rhode Island, South Carolina, South Dakota, Tennessee, Texas, Utah, Virginia, Washington State, West Virginia, Wisconsin, or Wyoming
$ Given: Approximately 50 awards of $1,000
   Deadline: February 15

ADDISON H. GIBSON FOUNDATION
1 PPG Place
Suite 2230
Pittsburgh, PA 15222
(412) 261-1611

Contact: Rebecca Wallace, Director
Restrictions: Residents of western Pennsylvania; only after one year of self-maintenance study
$ Loaned: Unavailable

G. WILLIAM KLEMSTINE FOUNDATION

c/o Pittsburgh National Bank C. & I. Trust Department
2 PNC Plaza, 620 Liberty Avenue, 25th floor
Pittsburgh, PA 15222-2719
(412) 762-7155

Contact: Brian Carroll
Restrictions: Residents of Cambria and Somerset counties in western Pennsylvania
$ Loaned: Unavailable

MARGARET AND IRVIN LESHER FOUNDATION SCHOLARSHIP

Lesher Foundation
P.O. Box 374
Oil City, PA 16301
(814) 677-5085

Contact: Barbara L. Staab, Administrator
Restrictions: Graduate of Union Joint School District high schools in Clarion County, PA; financial need; minimum 2.5 GPA for renewal
$ Given: 80 grants annually; $1,150 (four years), $1,500 (three years)
   Deadline: April 30

EDWIN T. MEREDITH FOUNDATION

Contact: Local County 4-H Office or State 4-H Office
Restrictions: Must be a 4-H member for at least one year; outstanding achievement; resident of Illinois, Indiana, Iowa, Kansas, Michigan, Minnesota, Missouri, Nebraska, New York, North Dakota, Ohio, Oklahoma, Pennsylvania, South Dakota, or Wisconsin
$ Given: Approximately three awards of $1,000
   Deadline: September 1

NEGRO EDUCATIONAL EMERGENCY DRIVE

Need Scholarship Program
Midtown Towers
643 Liberty Avenue
7th Floor
Pittsburgh, PA 15222
(412) 566-2760

Restrictions: Black; resident of Allegheny, Armstrong, Beaver, Butler, Washington, or Westmoreland counties, PA; high school diploma or GED
$ Given: 572 grants of $100–$1,000; renewable each year
   Deadline: April 30

PENNSYLVANIA DEPARTMENT OF MILITARY AFFAIRS
Bureau of Veterans Affairs (Scholarships)
Fort Indiantown Gap
Annville, PA 17003
(717) 861-8910

Contact: Esther Zellers
Restrictions: Resident of Pennsylvania five years prior to application; son or daughter (aged 16–23) whose parent died or was totally disabled as a result of war service in the U.S. armed forces; financial need
$ Given: Awards of $500; up to $4,000 over four years

PENNSYLVANIA HIGHER
EDUCATION ASSISTANCE AGENCY
Robert C. Byrd Scholarship
P.O. Box 8114
Harrisburg, PA 17105-8114
(717) 257-5220

Contact: Joan Lawhead, Coordinator for Teacher Education
Restrictions: Pennsylvania residents who meet two of these three requirements: rank in top 5% of class; minimum 3.5 GPA; or minimum 1100 combined SAT score or 27 composite ACT score; U.S. citizen. Age: 20 or under
$ Given: 275 awards for $1,500 each
   Deadline: May 1

PENNSYLVANIA HIGHER
EDUCATION ASSISTANCE AGENCY
State Higher Education Grants
1200 North Seventh Street
Harrisburg, PA 17102
(717) 257-2860 or (800) 692-7435

Restrictions: Resident of Pennsylvania and graduate of approved Pennsylvania secondary school or equivalent; enrolled full-time at an eligible U.S. institution for two years at least; financial need
$ Given: 80% of tuition and fees (not to exceed $2,632 in Pennsylvania or $600 out of state); renewable for four years
 Deadline: May 1

QUAKER CHEMICAL FOUNDATION

P.O. Box 809
Elm and Lee Streets
Conshohocken, PA 19428-0809
(215) 832-4101

Contact: Mary Lou McClain, Secretary to the Foundation
Restrictions: Children of Quaker Chemical employees
$ Given: Three to eight grants; range, $1,500–$4,000
 Deadline: December

SHANNON SCHOLARSHIP

Second Street & Howard Avenue
Pottsville, PA 17901
(717) 622-8720

Restrictions: Daughters of Episcopal priests residing in one of the five dioceses of Pennsylvania; freshman year
$ Given: 16 awards of $2,500
 Deadline: Must request application by April 15; application due back May 30

SICO FOUNDATION

15 Mount Joy
Mount Joy, PA 17552
(717) 653-1411

Contact: Dawn Zellers, Administrative Clerk
Restrictions: Delaware and some Pennsylvania and Maryland residents who are freshmen attending designated universities
$ Given: 120 grants of $1,000
 Deadline: February 15

HENRY E. AND FLORENCE
W. SNAYBERGER MEMORIAL FOUNDATION
c/o Pennsylvania National Bank and Trust Company
1 South Centre Street
Pottsville, PA 17901
(717) 622-4200

Contact: Lori Smith, Assistant Vice President and Trust Officer
Restrictions: Residents of Schuylkill County, PA
$ Given: Unavailable
   Deadline: February 28

ANNA M. VINCENT TRUST
c/o Mellon Bank (East)
Mellon Bank Center, P.O. Box 7899
Philadelphia, PA 19101-7899
(215) 553-3000

Contact: Pat Kling, Trust Officer
Restrictions: Residents of Delaware Valley area of Pennsylvania
$ Given: Unavailable
   Deadline: March 1

WILLIAMS (FRANK P. AND CLARA R.) SCHOLARSHIP
P.O. Box 374
Oil City, PA 16301
(814) 677-5085

Contact: Barbara Staab, Administrator
Restrictions: Graduates of high schools in Vanango County, PA; financial need; preference given to students of Allegheny College
$ Given: 150 grants annually; range, $100–$6,000
   Deadline: April 30

BENJAMIN AND FEDORA WOLF FOUNDATION
Park Towne Place–North Building 1205
Parkway at 22nd
Philadelphia, PA 19130
(215) 204-6079

Contact: David A. Horowitz, Administrator
Restrictions: Residents of Philadelphia, PA area; recommendation of high school principal or counselor required
$ Given: 196 grants totaling $81,175; range, $250–$625
   Deadline: June 1

RHODE ISLAND

MARJORIE SELLS CARTER TRUST
BOY SCOUT SCHOLARSHIP
P.O. Box 527
West Chatham, MA 02669
(508) 945-1225

Contact: Mrs. B.J. Shaffer
Restrictions: Boy scouts from one of six New England states (including Rhode Island) who has been active in scouting for at least two years; leadership ability; financial need
$ Given: Approximately 35 awards of $1,500
   Deadline: April 15

FFA WAL-MART SCHOLARSHIP
P.O. Box 15160
Alexandria, VA 22309-0160
(703) 360-3600

Restrictions: FFA member; freshman-year agriculture major; resident of Alabama, Arkansas, Arizona, California, Colorado, Connecticut, Delaware, Florida, Georgia, Hawaii, Idaho, Illinois, Indiana, Iowa, Kansas, Kentucky, Louisiana, Maine, Maryland, Michigan, Minnesota, Mississippi, Missouri, Montana, Nebraska, Nevada, New Hampshire, New Mexico, New York, North Carolina, North Dakota, Ohio, Oklahoma, Oregon, Pennsylvania, Puerto Rico, Rhode Island, South Carolina, South Dakota, Tennessee, Texas, Utah, Virginia, Washington State, West Virginia, Wisconsin, or Wyoming

$ Given: Approximately 50 awards of $1,000
    Deadline: February 15

MARY E. HODGES FUND
222 Taupton Avenue
E. Providence, RI 02914
(401) 435-4650

Contact: Grand Secretary
Restrictions: Residents of Rhode Island for minimum five years or Rhode Island Masonic affiliation; based on financial need and academic achievement
$ Given: Unavailable
    Deadline: Unavailable

RHODE ISLAND HIGHER EDUCATION
ASSISTANCE AUTHORITY
Grant and Scholarship Program
560 Jefferson Boulevard
Warwick, RI 02886
(401) 736-1100

Restrictions: Resident of Rhode Island enrolled at least half-time at an eligible postsecondary institution in U.S., Canada or Mexico; U.S. citizen or legal resident; financial need
$ Given: Unspecified number of grants of $250–$700, renewable yearly
    Deadline: March 1

RHODE ISLAND HIGHER EDUCATION
ASSISTANCE AUTHORITY
Stafford Loan Program
560 Jefferson Boulevard
Warwick, RI 02886
(401) 736-1100

Restrictions: Residents of Rhode Island; minimum half time enrollment; financial need; U.S. citizens or legal residents
$ Loaned: $2,625 freshmen; $3,500 sophomores; $5,500 juniors and seniors

SOUTH CAROLINA

AMERICAN LEGION ROBERT E. DAVID SCHOLARSHIP FOR THE CHILDREN OF VIETNAM AND KOREAN WAR VETERANS

American Legion, Department of South Carolina
P.O. Box 11355
Columbia, SC 29211-1355

Restrictions: South Carolina resident studying at South Carolina school; American Legion member or relative
$ Given: Approximately 20 awards of $500
    Deadline: May 1

THE DAVE CAMERON EDUCATIONAL FOUNDATION

P.O. Box 181
York, SC 29745
(803) 684-4968

Contact: John Adkins
Restrictions: York, SC, undergraduate students who maintain a minimum 2.0 GPA; based on financial need and academic achievement
$ Given: Range, $500–$2,000; four years, renewable yearly
    Deadline: May 1

CAROLINA SCHOLARS FINALIST AWARDS

University of South Carolina
1714 College Street
Columbia, SC 29208
(803) 777-8134

Contact: John Bannister, Director of Financial Aid
Restrictions: Students with leadership skills and academic merit
$ Given: 30 scholarships of varying amounts; average, $5,000
    Deadline: May 1

FFA WAL-MART SCHOLARSHIP

P.O. Box 15160Alexandria, VA 22309-0160
(703) 360-3600

Restrictions: FFA member; freshman-year agriculture major; resident of Alabama, Arkansas, Arizona, California, Colorado, Connecticut, Delaware, Florida, Georgia, Hawaii, Idaho, Illinois, Indiana, Iowa, Kansas, Kentucky, Louisiana, Maine, Maryland, Michigan, Minnesota, Mississippi, Missouri, Montana, Nebraska, Nevada, New Hampshire, New Mexico, New York, North Carolina, North Dakota, Ohio, Oklahoma, Oregon, Pennsylvania, Puerto Rico, Rhode Island, South Carolina, South Dakota, Tennessee, Texas, Utah, Virginia, Washington State, West Virginia, Wisconsin, or Wyoming
$ Given: Approximately 50 awards of $1,000
  Deadline: February 15

C.G. FULLER FOUNDATION
c/o Nations Bank of South Carolina
P.O. Box 448
Columbia, SC 29202
(803) 929-5879

Contact: Pamela S. Postal, Assistant Vice President
Restrictions: South Carolina residents attending colleges and universities in South Carolina; financial need and academic merit
$ Given: 15 grants of $1,000 per semester
  Deadline: March 31

NUCOR FOUNDATION, INC.
2100 Rexford Road
Charlotte, NC 28211
(704) 366-7000

Contact: Elizabeth Wells
Restrictions: Children of Nucor, Inc., employees only; must maintain 2.0 GPA in college
$ Given: Up to $2,200 per year for four years
  Deadline: March 1

PALMETTO FELLOWS SCHOLARSHIP
South Carolina Commission on Higher Education
1333 Main Street, Suite 200
Columbia, SC 29201

Contact: Dr. Karen Woodfaulk
Restrictions: South Carolina high school seniors attending South
Carolina schools
$ Given: $5,000, renewable
   Deadline: October 1

SOUTH CAROLINA DEPARTMENT OF VETERANS AFFAIRS

Governor's Office, Dept. of Veterans Affairs
1205 Pendleton Street, Room 226
Columbia, SC 29201
(803) 765-5104

Contact: Jimmie L. Gresham, Field Office Supervisor
Restrictions: Children of war veterans who were legal residents of South
Carolina at the time of their entry into the U.S. armed forces (or residents
for at least a year), and who were killed in action, died of disease, disability, or other causes resulting from service, or children of totally disabled veterans; age: 18 to 26; for undergraduate study at state-supported South Carolina institutions
$ Given: Unspecified number of tuition waivers
   Deadline: Set by the schools

SOUTH CAROLINA PRESS ASSOCIATION FOUNDATION
NEWSPAPER SCHOLARSHIP

P.O. Box 11429
Columbia, SC 29211
(803) 750-9561

Contact: Jennifer Roberts
Restrictions: Attend South Carolina college and be interested in a career
in newspapers; academic achievement; must participate in journalistic
activities in college. If recipient does not work in newspapers after graduation, grant becomes loan and must be repaid
$ Given: Three awards of $2,000–$2,500
   Deadline: June 1

SOUTH CAROLINA STATE STUDENT INCENTIVE GRANT

South Carolina Commission
on Higher Education
1333 Main Street, Suite 200
Columbia, SC 29201

Restrictions: Students attending South Carolina institutions; substantial financial need
$ Given: $2,000
　　Deadline: Varies by school

SOUTH CAROLINA TEACHER LOAN AND SOUTH CAROLINA GOVERNOR'S TEACHING SCHOLARSHIP LOAN

South Carolina Student Loan Corporation
P.O. Box 21487
Columbia, SC 29221

Contact: Ann Gregory
Restrictions: South Carolina residents attending South Carolina schools; must teach in a South Carolina public school in a critical-need area; 20% of loan forgiveness for each year taught
　　Deadline: May 15

SOUTH CAROLINA TUITION GRANTS COMMISSION

1310 Lady Street, Suite 811
P.O. Box 12159
Columbia, SC 29211-2159
(803) 734-1200

Restrictions: Residents of South Carolina for study in one of 20 South Carolina private colleges and universities; academic merit and financial need; U.S. citizens or permanent resident status
$ Given: 8,800 grants of $1,620–$3,420 (renewable)
　　Deadline: June 30

SOUTH DAKOTA

ROBERT C. BYRD HONORS SCHOLARSHIP

South Dakota Department of Education and Cultural Affairs
700 Governors Drive
Pierre, SD 57501-2291
(605) 773-3134

Restrictions: High school seniors; South Dakota residents; minimum 3.5 GPA and minimum ACT score of 24
$ Given: 20 awards of $1,500
  Deadline: May 1

FFA WAL-MART SCHOLARSHIP
P.O. Box 15160
Alexandria, VA 22309-0160
(703) 360-3600

Restrictions: FFA member; freshman-year agriculture major; resident of Alabama, Arkansas, Arizona, California, Colorado, Connecticut, Delaware, Florida, Georgia, Hawaii, Idaho, Illinois, Indiana, Iowa, Kansas, Kentucky, Louisiana, Maine, Maryland, Michigan, Minnesota, Mississippi, Missouri, Montana, Nebraska, Nevada, New Hampshire, New Mexico, New York, North Carolina, North Dakota, Ohio, Oklahoma, Oregon, Pennsylvania, Puerto Rico, Rhode Island, South Carolina, South Dakota, Tennessee, Texas, Utah, Virginia, Washington State, West Virginia, Wisconsin, or Wyoming
$ Given: Approximately 50 awards of $1,000
  Deadline: February 15

ANNIS I. FOWLER/KADEN SCHOLARSHIP
South Dakota Board of Regents
207 East Capitol Avenue
Pierre, SD 57501-3159

Restrictions: South Dakota high school seniors majoring in elementary education at a state South Dakota school; minimum 3.0 GPA
$ Given: $1,000
  Deadline: February 18

HAINES MEMORIAL SCHOLARSHIP
South Dakota Board of Regents
207 East Capitol Avenue
Pierre, SD 57501-3159

Restrictions: Sophomores, juniors, and seniors majoring at a state South Dakota school; minimum 2.5 GPA
$ Given: $1,750
  Deadline: February 18

EDWIN T. MEREDITH FOUNDATION

Contact: Local County 4-H Office or State 4-H Office
Restrictions: Must be a 4-H member for at least one year; outstanding achievement; resident of Illinois, Indiana, Iowa, Kansas, Michigan, Minnesota, Missouri, Nebraska, New York, North Dakota, Ohio, Oklahoma, Pennsylvania, South Dakota, or Wisconsin
$ Given: Approximately three awards of $1,000
    Deadline: September 1

SOUTH DAKOTA DEPARTMENT OF
EDUCATION AND CULTURAL AFFAIRS
State Student Incentive Grant
700 Governor's Drive
Pierre, SD 57501-2291
(605) 773-3134

Contact: Roxie Thielen
Restrictions: Residents of South Dakota attending approved South Dakota institutions on a minimum half-time basis; financial need
$ Given: Unavailable
    Deadline: Varies by institution

SOUTH DAKOTA DEPARTMENT OF
EDUCATION AND CULTURAL AFFAIRS
Tuition Equalization Grants (TEG Program)
700 Governor's Drive
Pierre, SD 57501-2291
(605) 773-3134

Contact: Roxie Thielen
Restrictions: Residents of South Dakota to attend approved South Dakota private colleges and universities; full-time; financial need; students may apply for both TEG and State Student Incentive grants but may accept only one.
$ Given: 500 grants annually; range, $100–$300; renewable
    Deadline: Varies by institution

SOUTH DAKOTA DIVISION OF VETERANS AFFAIRS
Aid to National Guardsmen
Department of Military and Veterans Affairs
44 East Capitol Avenue

Pierre, SD 57501-3185
(605) 336-3230

Restrictions: Residents of South Dakota who are active members of the South Dakota National Guard; for undergraduate studies at state-supported South Dakota colleges and universities
$ Given: Grants equal to 1/2 tuition; renewable yearly

TREACY COMPANY

Box 1700
Helena, MT 59624-1700
(406) 442-3632

Contact: James O'Connell
Restrictions: Residents of, or students attending, institutions in Idaho, Montana, North Dakota, and South Dakota; freshman or sophomore year
$ Given: 25 to 35 grants; average $400
   Deadline: June 15

TENNESSEE

AMERICAN LEGION ORATORICAL CONTEST

American Legion, Department of Tennessee
215 Eighth Avenue North
Nashville, TN 37203
(615) 254-0568

Restrictions: High school senior, Tennessee resident
$ Given: Approximately three awards, range, $1,500–$5,000
   Deadline: January 17

PAUL DOUGLAS TEACHER SCHOLARSHIP

Tennessee Student Assistance Corporation
404 James Robertson Parkway, Suite 1950
Nashville, TN 37243
(615) 741-1346

Restrictions: Tennessee resident who has graduated from a Tennessee

high school; minimum 3.0 GPA; must teach two years for each year award is received
$ Given: 10 awards, range, $1,000–$5,000
Deadline: March 1

FFA WAL-MART SCHOLARSHIP

P.O. Box 15160
Alexandria, VA 22309-0160
(703) 360-3600

Restrictions: FFA member; freshman-year agriculture major; resident of Alabama, Arkansas, Arizona, California, Colorado, Connecticut, Delaware, Florida, Georgia, Hawaii, Idaho, Illinois, Indiana, Iowa, Kansas, Kentucky, Louisiana, Maine, Maryland, Michigan, Minnesota, Mississippi, Missouri, Montana, Nebraska, Nevada, New Hampshire, New Mexico, New York, North Carolina, North Dakota, Ohio, Oklahoma, Oregon, Pennsylvania, Puerto Rico, Rhode Island, South Carolina, South Dakota, Tennessee, Texas, Utah, Virginia, Washington State, West Virginia, Wisconsin, or Wyoming
$ Given: Approximately 50 awards of $1,000
Deadline: February 15

NED MCWHERTER SCHOLARS PROGRAM

Tennessee Student Assistance Corporation
404 James Robertson Parkway, Suite 1950
Nashville, TN 37243
(615) 741-1346

Restrictions: Tennessee residents to attend Tennessee schools; 3.5 GPA and must score in top 5% on ACT or SAT
$ Given: Awards up to $6,000 per year for up to four years
Deadline: February 15

MINORITY TEACHING FELLOWS PROGRAM

Tennessee Student Assistance Corporation
404 James Robertson Parkway, Suite 1950
Nashville, TN 37243
(615) 741-1346

Contact: Michael C. Roberts
Restrictions: Tennessee residents from minority groups pursuing a teach-

ing career; for each year spent teaching one year of the loan will be for-given. Must be in top quarter of class.

$ Loaned: $5,000 per year for up to four years
    Deadline: May 15

TENNESSEE STUDENT ASSISTANCE CORPORATION

Student Assistance Awards
Parkway Towers
404 James Robertson Parkway
Suite 1950
Nashville, TN 37243-0820
(615) 741-1346

Contact: Ron Campbell
Restrictions: Residents of Tennessee; good academic standing at an accred-ited Tennessee institution; financial need; preference given to U.S. citizens
$ Given: 17,000 grants up to $2,682
    Deadline: May 1

UNIVERSITY OF TENNESSEE, KNOXVILLE

Neyland Scholarships
115 Student Services Building
Knoxville, TN 37994
(615) 974-7875 or 974-3131

Contact: Richard Bishop, Director of Financial Aid
Restrictions: Students of UTN, Knoxville; academic merit (rank in the top tenth of class) and leadership skills required; Tennessee resident or child of alumni
$ Given: Four awards of varying amounts; average, $1,200

TEXAS

ABILENE CHRISTIAN UNIVERSITY LEADERSHIP AWARDS

ACU Station, Box 29007
Abilene, TX 79699
(915) 674-2643

Contact: Stan Lambert, Director of Student Services

Restrictions: Students of academic merit
$ Given: Unspecified number; average, $2,000

AMARILLO AREA FOUNDATION, INC.
801 South Fillmore
Suite 700
Amarillo, TX 79101
(806) 376-4521

Contact: Sylvia Artho, Scholarship Coordinator
Restrictions: Residents of the 26 northernmost counties of the Texas Panhandle
$ Given: Unavailable
    Deadline: April 1

FAY T. BARNES SCHOLARSHIP TRUST
700 Lavaca
Austin, TX 78789-0001
(512) 479-2644

Contact: Regina Knouse, Assistant Administrator
Restrictions: Residents of Williamson and Travis counties, TX; must submit application through high school principal or counselor; financial need
$ Given: 10 grants totaling $239,750; range, $1,250–$2,500
    Deadline: January 1

ROBERT C. BYRD HONORS SCHOLARSHIP
Capitol Station
P.O. Box 12788
Austin, TX 78711-2788
(512) 483-6340

Contact: Gustavo DeLeon
Restrictions: Freshman year awards determined by GPA, class standing, and test scores
$ Given: Approximately 450 awards of $1,500
    Deadline: March 15

CHINESE PROFESSIONAL CLUB OF HOUSTON SCHOLARSHIP
11302 Fallbrook Drive
Houston, TX 77065
(713) 955-0115

Contact: James Tang, M.D. Scholarship Committee Chairman
Restrictions: Residents of Houston, TX, metropolitan area who are individuals of Chinese descent
$ Given: 10 awards, range, $600–$1,500
   Deadline: November 15

THE EL PASO COMMUNITY FOUNDATION

201 East Main Street, Suite 1616
El Paso, TX 79901
(915) 533-4020

Contact: Janet Windle
Restrictions: Residents of El Paso, TX, area
   $ Given: Unspecified number and amount

FFA WAL-MART SCHOLARSHIP

P.O. Box 15160
Alexandria, VA 22309-0160
(703) 360-3600

Restrictions: FFA member; freshman-year agriculture major; resident of Alabama, Arkansas, Arizona, California, Colorado, Connecticut, Delaware, Florida, Georgia, Hawaii, Idaho, Illinois, Indiana, Iowa, Kansas, Kentucky, Louisiana, Maine, Maryland, Michigan, Minnesota, Mississippi, Missouri, Montana, Nebraska, Nevada, New Hampshire, New Mexico, New York, North Carolina, North Dakota, Ohio, Oklahoma, Oregon, Pennsylvania, Puerto Rico, Rhode Island, South Carolina, South Dakota, Tennessee, Texas, Utah, Virginia, Washington State, West Virginia, Wisconsin, or Wyoming
$ Given: Approximately 50 awards of $1,000
   Deadline: February 15

D. D. HACHAR CHARITABLE TRUST FUND

c/o Laredo National Bank
P.O. Box 59
Laredo, TX 78044
(956) 723-1151

Contact: Trust Administrator
Restrictions: Residents of Laredo and Webb counties, TX
$ Given: 183 grants totaling $182,500; range, $500–$4,000
   Deadlines: Last Friday in April and October

GEORGE AND MARY JOSEPHINE HAMMAN FOUNDATION
910 Travis
Suite 1990
Houston, TX 77002-5816
(713) 658-8345

Contact: Allan Fritsche
Restrictions: Houston, TX, area high school seniors
$ Given: 30 grants totaling $10,000
    Deadline: February 28

ED E. AND GLADYS HURLEY FOUNDATION
c/o Bank One
P.O. Box 21116
Shreveport, LA 71154
(318) 226-2110

Contact: Monette Holler
Restrictions: Loans to residents of Arkansas, Louisiana, and Texas to attend institution of their choice
$ Loaned: Unavailable
    Deadline: May 31

HARRIS AND ELIZA KEMPNER FUND
2201 Market Street, Suite 601
Galveston, TX 77550
(409) 762-1603

Contact: Elaine Peruschio, Executive Director
Restrictions: Local high school seniors who will attend Galveston College or students attending College of The Mainland or Texas A&M at Galveston
$ Loaned: $3,000; renewable
    Deadline: March 31

ANN LANE SCHOLARSHIP
P.O. Box 9589
Austin, TX 78766-9589
(512) 454-0311

Contact: Dennis Engelke
Restrictions: Texas resident attending Texas school; active member of

Future Homemakers of America; financial need
$ Given: $1,000
    Deadline: March 1

FRANKLIN LINDSAY STUDENT AID FUND

Chase Bank of Texas
P.O. Box 550
Austin, TX 78789-0001
(512) 479-2444

Contact: Jean Parks
Restrictions: Students attending Texas colleges and universities; must maintain at least 2.0 GPA
$ Loaned: 350 loans of varying amounts up to $3,000

BRUCE MCMILLAN JR. FOUNDATION, INC.

P.O. Box 9
Overton, TX 75684
(903) 834-3148

Contact: Ralph Ward Jr., President
Restrictions: Students at eight high schools in the Overton, Texas, area
$ Given: Grants amounts vary

THE MOODY FOUNDATION

2302 Post Office Street
Suite 704
Galveston, TX 77550
(409) 763-5333

Contact: Sandy Griffin
Restrictions: Galveston County seniors to attend Texas colleges and universities
$ Given: Unavailable

NUCOR FOUNDATION, INC.

2100 Rexford Road
Charlotte, NC 28211
(704) 366-7000

Contact: Elizabeth Wells, Administrator

Restrictions: Children of Nucor, Inc., employees only; must maintain 2.0 GPA in college
$ Given: Up to $2,200 per year for four years
Deadline: March 1

ORATORICAL CONTEST SCHOLARSHIPS
P.O. Box 789
Austin, TX 78767
(512) 472-4138

Contact: Kerry Hall
Restrictions: High school senior, Texas resident; sponsored by an American Legion Post, and a state contest winner
$ Given: Four awards, range, $250–$1,000
Deadline: November 1

PRESS CLUB OF DALLAS FOUNDATION SCHOLARSHIPS
400 North Olive, LB 218
Dallas, TX 75201
(214) 740-9988

Contact: Carol Wortham
Restrictions: Attend Texas school, majoring in journalism, communications, or public relations; financial need
$ Given: 10 awards, range, $500–$2,000
Deadline: May 1

C. L. ROWAN CHARITABLE AND EDUCATIONAL FUND, INC.
1204-B West Seventh Street
Fort Worth, TX 76102
(817) 332-2327

Contact: Brent Rowan Hyder
Restrictions: Texas residents attending Texas universities; application by letter only
$ Given: Five grants averaging $1,000
Deadline: October 31

ROBERT SCHRECK MEMORIAL EDUCATIONAL FUND
Texas Commerce Bank–El Paso
P.O. Drawer 140

El Paso, TX 79980
(915) 546-6500

Contact: Terry Crenshaw, Charitable Services Officer
Restrictions: Students from El Paso County, TX; two years residence at least; studying theology, medicine, veterinary medicine, physics, chemistry, engineering, or architecture; must have completed two years of college
$ Given: Eight grants totaling $5,500; range, $500–$1,000
  Deadlines: July 15, November 15

THE ABE AND ANNIE SEIBEL FOUNDATION

c/o United States National Bank
P.O. Box 8210
Galveston, TX 77553-8210
(409) 763-1151

Contact: Judith T. Whelton, Trust Director
Restrictions: Graduates of Texas high schools attending Texas colleges and universities
$ Loaned: 750 loans totaling $1,500,000; range, $250–$3,000
  Deadline: February 28

THE M. L. SHANOR FOUNDATION

P.O. Box 7522
Wichita Falls, TX 76307
(817) 761-2401

Contact: J. B. Jarratt, President
Restrictions: Primarily local giving
$ Loaned: 63 loans totaling $95,025; range, $275–$2,500
  Deadline: August 1

STATE SCHOLARSHIP PROGRAM
FOR ETHNIC RECRUITMENT

Texas Higher Education Coordinating Board,
Tuition Exemption
P.O. Box 12788
Capitol Station
Austin, TX 78711-2788
(512) 483-6100

Restrictions: Minority students whose ethnic group makes up less than 40% of the student body at the school recipient is attending; freshmen and

transfer students; financial need, academic merit
$ Given: $2,000

STATE STUDENT INCENTIVE GRANT
Texas Higher Education Coordinating Board,
Tuition Exemption
P.O. Box 12788
Capitol Station
Austin, TX 78711-2788
(512) 483-6100

Restrictions: Students attending state schools in Texas; do not have to be residents; financial need
$ Given: Unavailable

SUNNYSIDE, INC.
8222 Douglas Avenue, Suite 501
Dallas, TX 75225
(214) 692-5686

Contact: Nadine Givens, Executive Director
Restrictions: Residents of Texas age 21 or under with financial need; must attend Christian Science Sunday school
$ Given: 18 grants totaling $29,000; range $500–$4,000

TEXAS HISTORY ESSAY CONTEST
5942 Abrams Road, #222
Dallas, TX 75231
(214) 343-2146

Contact: Maydee J. Scurlock
Restrictions: Applicant must write an essay on Texas history and how it influenced the development of Texas.
$ Given: Three awards; range, $1,000–$3,000
  Deadline: February 6

TEXAS PUBLIC EDUCATIONAL GRANT
Texas Higher Education Coordinating Board, Tuition Exemption
P.O. Box 12788

Capitol Station
Austin, TX 78711-2788
(512) 483-6100

Restrictions: Students attending state schools in Texas; financial need; do not have to be residents of Texas
$ Given: Award amounts are determined by the financial aid office of each individual school; renewable
    Deadline: Varies

TUITION EQUALIZATION GRANT
Texas Higher Education Coordinating Board, Tuition Exemption
P.O. Box 12788
Capitol Station
Austin, TX 78711-2788
(512) 483-6100

Restrictions: Texas residents attending private Texas schools; financial need
$ Given: Awards to $2,640
    Deadline: Varies by school

UTD PRESIDENTIAL
University of Texas at Dallas
P.O. Box 830688 MC-12
Richardson, TX 75083-0688
(972) 690-2941

Contact: Michael Rear, Director of Financial Aid
Restrictions: Students of African-American or Hispanic descent
$ Given: Unspecified number of grants in varying amounts

VETERANS AND DEPENDENTS TUITION EXEMPTION
Texas Higher Education Coordinating Board,
Tuition Exemption
P.O. Box 12788
Capitol Station
Austin, TX 78711-2788
(512) 483-6100

Contact: Jane Caldwell

Restrictions: Texas veteran or child of deceased Texas veteran; attend state school in Texas
$ Given: Approximately 9,500 awards of $550

CLARA STEWART WATSON FOUNDATION
c/o Nations Bank
P.O. Box 830241
Dallas, TX 75283
(214) 559-6321

Contact: Mary Dell Green
Restrictions: Graduates of Dallas and Tarrant counties, TX, high schools to study at Texas colleges and universities
$ Loaned: 10–12 scholarships of $1,000 each
  Deadline: Write to bank in January; final deadline March 15

THE DAVID AND EULA WINTERMAN FOUNDATION
P.O. Box 337
Eagle Lake, TX 77434
(409) 234-5551

Restrictions: High school seniors who intend to study medicine; must attend high school in Rice Consolidated School District
$ Given: Three grants totaling $4,000; range, $1,000–$2,000
  Deadline: April

UTAH

RUTH ELEANOR AND JOHN ERNEST BAMBERGER MEMORIAL FOUNDATION
136 South Main Street, Suite 418
Salt Lake City, UT 84101
(801) 364-2045

Contact: William H. Olwell, Secretary-Treasurer
Restrictions: Utah residents, with preference given to student nurses
$ Given: Unavailable

FFA WAL-MART SCHOLARSHIP
P.O. Box 15160
Alexandria, VA 22309-0160
(703) 360-3600

Restrictions: FFA member; freshman-year agriculture major; resident of Alabama, Arkansas, Arizona, California, Colorado, Connecticut, Delaware, Florida, Georgia, Hawaii, Idaho, Illinois, Indiana, Iowa, Kansas, Kentucky, Louisiana, Maine, Maryland, Michigan, Minnesota, Mississippi, Missouri, Montana, Nebraska, Nevada, New Hampshire, New Mexico, New York, North Carolina, North Dakota, Ohio, Oklahoma, Oregon, Pennsylvania, Puerto Rico, Rhode Island, South Carolina, South Dakota, Tennessee, Texas, Utah, Virginia, Washington State, West Virginia, Wisconsin, or Wyoming
$ Given: Approximately 50 awards of $1,000
   Deadline: February 15

NUCOR FOUNDATION, INC.
2100 Rexford Road
Charlotte, NC 28211
(704) 366-7000

Contact: Elizabeth Wells, Administrator
Restrictions: Children of Nucor, Inc., employees only; must maintain 2.0 GPA in college
$ Given: Up to $2,200 per year for four years
   Deadline: March 1

VERMONT

MARJORIE SELLS CARTER TRUST
BOY SCOUT SCHOLARSHIP
P.O. Box 527
West Chatham, MA 02669
(508) 945-1225

Contact: Mrs. B. J. Shaffer

Restrictions: Must be a Boy Scout from one of six New England states including Vermont; active in scouting for at least two years; leadership ability, financial need
$ Given: Approximately 35 awards of $1,500
    Deadline: April 15

FAUGHT MEMORIAL SCHOLARSHIPS

Vermont Community Foundation
P.O. Box 30
Middlebury, VT 05753
(802) 388-3355

Contact: Lynn Dunton, Director
Restrictions: Students at Union High School, District 27, Bellows Falls, VT
$ Given: Three grants of $400 each
    Deadline: Varies

OLIN SCOTT FUND, INC.

407 Main
P.O. Box 1208
Bennington, VT 05201
(802) 447-1096

Contact: Melvin A. Dyson, President
Restrictions: Young men in Bennington County, VT; minimum 2.5 GPA
$ Loaned: Average loan $3,000–$12,000 over four years

UNIVERSITY OF VERMONT SCHOLARSHIPS

330 Waterman
South Prospect Street
Burlington, VT 05401
(802) 656-3156

Contact: Donald Honemane, Director
Restrictions: UVT students with academic merit; financial need
$ Given: Unspecified number of awards

VERMONT PART-TIME STUDENT GRANTS

Vermont Student Assistance Corporation
Champlain Mill

P.O. Box 2000
Winooski, VT 05404-2601

Restrictions: Vermont residents taking fewer than 12 credits per semester; financial need
$ Given: Not available

VERMONT STUDENT ASSISTANCE CORPORATION

Guaranteed Student Loans
Champlain Mill
P.O. Box 2000
Winooski, VT 05404-2000
(802) 655-9602

Restrictions: Residents of Vermont U.S. citizens or permanent residents
$ Loaned: Unspecified number of loans; range, $2,625–$5,500; renewable

VERMONT STUDENT ASSISTANCE CORPORATION

Incentive Grants
Champlain Mill
P.O. Box 2000
Winooski, VT 05404-2000
(802) 655-9602

Restrictions: Residents of Vermont for minimum one year; high school graduate or equivalent to attend approved postsecondary Vermont institution for undergraduate study; financial need; U.S. citizen or legal resident
$ Given: 8,500 grants per year; range, $400–$5,200
   Deadline: March 31

THE WINDHAM FOUNDATION

P.O. Box 70
Grafton, VT 05146
(802) 843-2211

Contact: Stephen A. Morse, President
Restrictions: Windham County, VT residents
$ Given: Awards totaling about $150,000
   Deadline: April 1

VIRGINIA

ETHEL N. BOWEN FOUNDATION, INC.
c/o First National Bank of Bluefield
P.O. Box 1559
Bluefield, WV 24701
(304) 325-8181

Contact: R. W. Wilkinson, Secretary-Treasurer
Restrictions: Students top tenth of their class, from southern West Virginia and southwestern Virginia coalfields
$ Given: 20 grants
   Deadline: April 30

CAMP FOUNDATION
P.O. Box 813
Franklin, VA 23851
(804) 562-3439

Contact: Harold S. Atkinson, Executive Director
Restrictions: High school graduates or residents from Southampton, Isle of Wight, or Franklin Counties, VA
$ Given: Seven scholarships per year totaling $19,000
   Deadlines: February 26 for filing with principals; March 15 for principals to file with the foundation

PAUL DOUGLAS TEACHER SCHOLARSHIP
James Monroe Building
101 North 14th Street
Richmond, VA 23219
(804) 786-1690

Restrictions: Virginia resident attending school in Virginia; rank in top 10% of class; must teach two years for each year of money received
$ Given: $5,000

FFA WAL-MART SCHOLARSHIP
P.O. Box 15160
Alexandria, VA 22309-0160
(703) 360-3600

Restrictions: FFA member; freshman-year agriculture major; resident of Alabama, Arkansas, Arizona, California, Colorado, Connecticut, Delaware, Florida, Georgia, Hawaii, Idaho, Illinois, Indiana, Iowa, Kansas, Kentucky, Louisiana, Maine, Maryland, Michigan, Minnesota, Mississippi, Missouri, Montana, Nebraska, Nevada, New Hampshire, New Mexico, New York, North Carolina, North Dakota, Ohio, Oklahoma, Oregon, Pennsylvania, Puerto Rico, Rhode Island, South Carolina, South Dakota, Tennessee, Texas, Utah, Virginia, Washington State, West Virginia, Wisconsin, or Wyoming
$ Given: Approximately 50 awards of $1,000
Deadline: February 15

ORATORICAL CONTEST SCHOLARSHIP
1805 Chantilly Street
Richmond, VA 23230
(804) 353-6606

Restrictions: Virginia high school seniors who win the Virginia department oratorical contest
$ Given: Three awards, range, $600–$1,100
Deadline: December 1

VIRGINIA STATE COUNCIL OF HIGHER EDUCATION
College Scholarship Assistance Program
101 North 14th Street, James Monroe Building
Richmond, VA 23219
(804) 371-0553

Contact: Zita Barree
Restrictions: Resident of Virginia; for at least half-time undergraduate study at an eligible Virginia college or university; financial need; not enrolled in a religious program
$ Given: Unspecified number of grants of $400–$2,000
Deadline: Varies

VIRGINIA STATE COUNCIL OF HIGHER EDUCATION
Tuition Assistance Grant Program
101 North 14th Street, James Monroe Building
Richmond, VA 23219
(804) 225-2141

Restrictions: Resident of Virginia; for full-time (undergraduate) study at an eligible private institution in Virginia, apply at financial aid office; can't be used for religious study
$ Given.   Unspecified number of grants up to $1,500; renewable to four years for undergraduates
   Deadline: July 31

VIRGINIA STATE COUNCIL OF HIGHER EDUCATION
Virginia Transfer Grant Program
101 North 14th Street, James Monroe Building
Richmond, VA 23219
(804) 225-2141

Contact: Melissa Collin
Restrictions: Resident of Virginia; member of a racial minority; for full- and half-time study at a public Virginia college or university; whites transfering to Norfolk State of Virginia State Colleges, must live in Virginia; must meet minimum merit criteria
$ Given: Unspecified number of grants, up to full tuition, including fees.
   Deadline: Set by institutions

MARK AND CATHERINE WINKLER FOUNDATION
4900 Seminary Road, Suite 900
Alexandria, VA 22311
(703) 998-0400

Contact: Lynn Ball, Executive Director
Restrictions: Residents of Virginia who are single parents
$ Given: Unavailable

WASHINGTON STATE

AMERICAN INDIAN ENDOWED SCHOLARSHIP
Washington Higher Education Coordinating Board
917 Lakeridge Way
P.O. Box 43430
Olympia, WA 98504-3430

Contact: Barbara Theiss, Program Manager
Restrictions: Washington resident; American Indian; financial need
$ Given: Three awards of $1,000

AWARDS OF EXCELLENCE
Pacific Coca-Cola
1150 124th Avenue, Northeast
P.O. Box C-93346
Bellevue, WA 98009-3346
(206) 455-2000

Contact: Terry Conner, Key Account Representative
Restrictions: Graduates of high schools in western Washington, Yakima, and Wenatchee areas planning to enroll in the following participating colleges: Pacific Lutheran University, Seattle Pacific University, Seattle University, Saint Martin's College, University of Puget Sound, The Evergreen State College, University of Washington, and Western Washington University; minimum high school GPA of 3.5. Students should apply directly to Admissions Director of chosen college for funding consideration.
$ Given: 18 grants; average, $1,500
Deadline: Mid-April

NELLIE MARTIN CARMAN SCHOLARSHIP TRUST
c/o Key Trust Company National Association
P.O. Box 12907
Seattle, WA 98111
(206) 684-6153

Contact: Secretary, Scholarship Committee
Restrictions: King, Snohomish, and Pierce counties, WA, high school graduates who will attend colleges in Washington; by school nomination only
$ Given: Awards of $500, $750, and $1,000

EDUCATIONAL OPPORTUNITY GRANT
Washington Higher Education Coordinating Board
917 Lakeridge Way
P.O. Box 43430
Olympia, WA 98504-3430

Contact: Barbara Theiss, Program Manager
Restrictions: Students who have completed an associate degree or its

equivalent; financial need; must be a resident of one of 14 designated counties in Washington State
$ Given: 200 awards of $2,500
> **Deadline:** June 1

FFA WAL-MART SCHOLARSHIP
P.O. Box 15160
Alexandria, VA 22309-0160
(703) 360-3600

Restrictions: FFA member; freshman-year agriculture major; resident of Alabama, Arkansas, Arizona, California, Colorado, Connecticut, Delaware, Florida, Georgia, Hawaii, Idaho, Illinois, Indiana, Iowa, Kansas, Kentucky, Louisiana, Maine, Maryland, Michigan, Minnesota, Mississippi, Missouri, Montana, Nebraska, Nevada, New Hampshire, New Mexico, New York, North Carolina, North Dakota, Ohio, Oklahoma, Oregon, Pennsylvania, Puerto Rico, Rhode Island, South Carolina, South Dakota, Tennessee, Texas, Utah, Virginia, Washington State, West Virginia, Wisconsin, or Wyoming

$ Given: Approximately 50 awards of $1,000
> **Deadline:** February 15

PAUL L. FOWLER MEMORIAL SCHOLARSHIP
Washington Higher Education
Coordinating Board
917 Lakeridge Way
P.O. Box 43430
Olympia, WA 98504-3430

Contact: Ms. Ann McLendon
Restrictions: High school Washington State senior; for use in freshman year
$ Given: Nine awards of $3,000
> **Deadline:** March 22

KCPQ-TV-EWING C. KELLY SCHOLARSHIP
4400 Steilacoom Blvd. SW
P.O. Box 98828
Tacoma, WA 98499-4002
(206) 625-1313

Contact: Keith Shipman
Restrictions: High school senior living within KCPQ's viewing area in Washington State (Seattle-Tacoma area); must have minimum composite score of 20 on ACT or minimum combined score on SAT of 840
$ Given: $2,000
   Deadline: February 15

NEED GRANT PROGRAM

Washington Higher Education Coordinating Board
917 Lakeridge Way
P.O. Box 43430
Olympia, WA 98504-3430

Contact: Terri May
Restrictions: Washington residents attending Washington schools; financial need
$ Given: Approximately 42,000 awards of varying amounts

PACIFIC PRINTING AND IMAGING ASSOCIATION

Educational Trust Scholarships
180 Nickerson, Suite 102
Seattle, WA 98109

Contact: Jim Olsen
Restrictions: Students studying printing, print management, or graphic arts technology; must live in Washington, Oregon, Arkansas, Idaho, Montana, or Hawaii
$ Given: 12 awards, range, $500–$2,500; renewable
   Deadline: April 1

ARTHUR AND DOREEN PARRETT
SCHOLARSHIP TRUST FUND

c/o U.S. Bank of Washington N.A.
P.O. Box 720, Trust Division-W-WH 271
Seattle, WA 98111-0720
(206) 344-3685or (800) 505-4545

Contact: Alexandra Rumbaugh, Trust Officer
Restrictions: Residents of Washington to study engineering, science, medicine, and dentistry; must have completed one year of college; U.S. citizen

$ Given: 15 to 20 grants; range, $1,500–$2,500
    Deadline: July 31

GEORGE T. WELCH TESTAMENTARY TRUST
c/o Baker-Boyer National Bank
P.O. Box 1796
Walla Walla, WA 99362
(509) 525-2000

Contact: Holly T. Howard, Trust Officer
Restrictions: Unmarried residents of Walla Walla County, WA; financial need
$ Given: 60 grants totaling $88,000; range, $1,000–$2,500
    Deadline: April 1

WASHINGTON SCHOLARS
Washington Higher Education Coordinating Board
917 Lakeridge Way
P.O. Box 43430
Olympia, WA 98504-3430

Contact: Ann McLendon
Restrictions: High school seniors who are in top 1% of graduating class; minimum 3.3 GPA; must be nominated by high school principals

WEST VIRGINIA

ETHEL N. BOWEN FOUNDATION, INC.
c/o First National Bank of Bluefield
P.O. Box 1559
Bluefield, WV 24701
(304) 325-8181

Contact: R. W. Wilkinson, Secretary-Treasurer
Restrictions: Students in the top tenth of their class from southern West Virginia and southwestern Virginia coalfields
$ Given: 20 grants; range, $500–$5,000
    Deadline: April 30

PAUL DOUGLAS TEACHER SCHOLARSHIP

Central Office of the State College and University System
P.O. Box 4007
Charleston, WV 25364-4007

Contact: Daniel Crockett
Restrictions: West Virginia resident, rank in top 10% of class, majoring in a program leading to teacher certification; must teach for two years for each year of monies received, otherwise scholarship becomes loan with interest.
$ Given: Up to $5,000
    Deadline: April 1

FFA WAL-MART SCHOLARSHIP

P.O. Box 15160
Alexandria, VA 22309-0160
(703) 360-3600

Restrictions: FFA member; freshman-year agriculture major; resident of Alabama, Arkansas, Arizona, California, Colorado, Connecticut, Delaware, Florida, Georgia, Hawaii, Idaho, Illinois, Indiana, Iowa, Kansas, Kentucky, Louisiana, Maine, Maryland, Michigan, Minnesota, Mississippi, Missouri, Montana, Nebraska, Nevada, New Hampshire, New Mexico, New York, North Carolina, North Dakota, Ohio, Oklahoma, Oregon, Pennsylvania, Puerto Rico, Rhode Island, South Carolina, South Dakota, Tennessee, Texas, Utah, Virginia, Washington State, West Virginia, Wisconsin, or Wyoming
$ Given: Approximately 50 awards of $1,000
    Deadline: February 15

THE GREATER KANAWHA VALLEY FOUNDATION

P.O. Box 3041
Charleston, WV 25331
(304) 346-3620

Contact: Betsy V. VonBlond, Executive Director
Restrictions: West Virginia residents, affiliated with Mountaineer Gas Company; U.S. citizen; academic achievement (at least 2.5 GPA)
$ Given: 250 grants totaling $500,000
    Deadline: February 14

JAMES HARLESS FOUNDATION, INC.
P.O. Box 1210
Gilbert, WV 25621
(304) 664-3227

Restrictions: Residents of Gilbert, WV, area
$ Loaned: About $5,000

HERSCHEL C. PRICE EDUCATIONAL FOUNDATION
P.O. Box 412
Huntington, WV 25708-0412
(304) 529-3852

Restrictions: West Virginia students or students attending West Virginia schools who show financial need and scholarship standing
$ Given: Unavailable

GEORGE E. STIFEL SCHOLARSHIP FUND
c/o Bank One, WV Wheeling, N.A.
P.O. Box 511
Wheeling, WV 26003
(304) 233-0600

Contact: Ed Johnson, Senior Trust Officer
Restrictions: Residents of Ohio County, WV, ages 17–25, graduates of Wheeling, WV high schools; financial need; good academic standing (at least B average)
$ Given: 45 grants; range, $1,000–$2,600
   Deadline: March 1

UNDERWOOD-SMITH TEACHER SCHOLARSHIP PROGRAM
Central Office of the State College and University System
P.O. Box 4007
Charleston, WV 25364-4007

Restrictions: West Virginia resident attending West Virginia school; education program; graduate in top 10% of high school class, score in top 10% on ACT or have college GPA of 3.25; must teach for two years for each year of money received
$ Given: Up to $5,000
   Deadline: April 1

WEST VIRGINIA HIGHER EDUCATION FOUNDATION
Robert C. Byrd Honors Scholarship
State College and University Systems
1018 Kanawha Boulevard East, Suite 700
Charleston, WV 25301
(304) 347-1266

Contact: Diana P. Wood, Financial Aid Administration
Restrictions: High school graduates demonstrating outstanding academic achievements; students must apply through their high school guidance counselors; age: 20 or under
$ Given: 135 grants
   Deadline: March 15

WEST VIRGINIA ITALIAN HERITAGE
FESTIVAL SCHOLARSHIP
1860 19th Street NW
Washington, D.C. 20009-5599
(202) 638-2137

Contact: Dr. Maria Lombardo, Education Director
Restrictions: Italian-American West Virginia resident; financial need
$ Given: Approximately four awards of $625
   Deadline: May 31

WEST VIRGINIA STATE COLLEGE
AND UNIVERSITY SYSTEMS
West Virginia Higher Education Grant Program
P.O. Box 4007
Charleston, WV 25364-4007
(304) 347-1211

Contact: Robert A. Cong, Grants Program Coordinator
Restrictions: Resident of West Virginia or Pennsylvania one year prior to application; high school graduate enrolled as full-time undergraduate at an approved West Virginia institution; financial need
$ Given: 5,000 grants per year; range, $350–$2,136; reapplication necessary
   Deadlines: January 1, March 1

WISCONSIN

AMERICAN LEGION,
DEPARTMENT OF WISCONSIN
812 East State Street
Milwaukee, WI 53202

Restrictions: High school senior, Wisconsin residents
$ Given: Six awards of $250–$500

FFA WAL-MART SCHOLARSHIP
P.O. Box 15160
Alexandria, VA 22309-0160
(703) 360-3600

Restrictions: FFA member; freshman-year agriculture major; resident of Alabama, Arkansas, Arizona, California, Colorado, Connecticut, Delaware, Florida, Georgia, Hawaii, Idaho, Illinois, Indiana, Iowa, Kansas, Kentucky, Louisiana, Maine, Maryland, Michigan, Minnesota, Mississippi, Missouri, Montana, Nebraska, Nevada, New Hampshire, New Mexico, New York, North Carolina, North Dakota, Ohio, Oklahoma, Oregon, Pennsylvania, Puerto Rico, Rhode Island, South Carolina, South Dakota, Tennessee, Texas, Utah, Virginia, Washington State, West Virginia, Wisconsin, or Wyoming
$ Given: Approximately 50 awards of $1,000
   Deadline: February 15

GUY STANTON FORD
EDUCATIONAL FOUNDATION INC.
119 Martin Luther King, Jr. Boulevard
Madison, WI 53703
(608) 257-4812

Contact: Jack D. Walker, Treasurer
Restrictions: Members of Sigma Deuteron Charge of Theta Delta Chi Fraternity attending University of Wisconsin at Madison; eligibility determined by the fraternity
$ Given: 16 grants totaling $2,096; range, $37–$491

JANESVILLE FOUNDATION, INC.

121 North Parker Drive
P.O. Box 8123
Janesville, WI 53427-8123
(608) 752-1032

Contact: Bonnie Lynne Robinson
Restrictions: High school seniors attending Janesville high schools
$ Given: Grants at $2,000 and at $1,000 per year for four years

KOHLER FOUNDATION, INC.

1725 X Woodlake Road
Kohler, WI 53044
(920) 458-1972

Contact: Deborah Hufford, Executive Director
Restrictions: Sheboygan County high school seniors recommended by their schools
$ Given: Unavailable

LA CROSSE COMMUNITY FOUNDATION

319 Main Street, Suite 301
La Crosse, WI 54601-0708
(608) 782-3223

Contact: Sheila Garrity, Program Director
Restrictions: Residents of La Crosse, WI, chosen by La Crosse County schools
$ Given: Unavailable

EDWIN T. MEREDITH FOUNDATION

Contact: Local County 4-H Office or State 4-H Office
Restrictions: Must be a 4-H member for at least one year; outstanding achievement; resident of Illinois, Indiana, Iowa, Kansas, Michigan, Minnesota, Missouri, Nebraska, New York, North Dakota, Ohio, Oklahoma, Pennsylvania, South Dakota, or Wisconsin
$ Given: Approximately three awards of $1,000
Deadline: September 1

MILWAUKEE MUSIC SCHOLARSHIP FOUNDATION
c/o First Wisconsin Trust Company
P.O. Box 2054
Milwaukee, WI 53201
(920) 765-5123

Contact: Mrs. Jewal A. Graff
Restrictions: Music student ages 16–26; Wisconsin resident;
financial need
$ Given: Approximately four awards, range, $500–$1,000
   Deadline: February 1

ORATORICAL CONTEST SCHOLARSHIP
Department Headquarters
812 East State Street
Milwaukee, WI 53202

Restrictions: State or regional high school oratorical contest winner
$ Given: 12 awards, range, $300–$1,000

OSHKOSH FOUNDATION
404 North Main
P.O. Box 1726
Oshkosh, WI 54902
(920) 426-3993

Contact: R. Andrew Sweeney
Restrictions: Graduating high school seniors; Oshkosh residents
$ Given: Unavailable

EDWARD RUTHLEDGE CHARITY
404 North Bridge Street, P.O. Box 758
Chippewa Falls, WI 54729
(715) 723-6618

Contact: Gerald J. Naiberg, President
Restrictions: Chippewa County, WI, residents
$ Given: Unavailable
   Deadline: July 1

TALENT INCENTIVE PROGRAM

Wisconsin Educational Opportunity
101 West Pleasant Street
Milwaukee, WI 53212

Restrictions: Wisconsin residents attending Wisconsin schools; financial need
$ Given: $600–$1,800

WISCONSIN ACADEMIC EXCELLENCE SCHOLARSHIP

Wisconsin Higher Education Board
P.O. Box 7885
Madison, WI 53707-7885

Restrictions: Graduating high school seniors who have the highest GPA; attend Wisconsin school; must be enrolled full time and maintain a 3.0 GPA
$ Given: Full tuition and related fees for up to four years

WISCONSIN DEPARTMENT OF VETERAN AFFAIRS

Educational Grant and Loan Programs
P.O. Box 7843
Madison, WI 53707-7843
(608) 266-1311

Contact: Local veteran's service offices or school financial aid offices
Restrictions: Dependent children or unmarried spouses of deceased veterans or veterans who are Wisconsin residents and served during wartime or in an armed conflict; the veterans themselves are to be unemployed and show financial need.
$ Given: Approximately 9,000 grants and loans per year; $3,000 maxmum
Deadline: 60 days after end of semester

WISCONSIN HIGHER EDUCATION AIDS BOARD

Grant Program
P.O. Box 7885
Madison, WI 53707-7885
(608) 267-2206

Contact: High school counselor

Restrictions: Resident of Wisconsin, enrolled at least half-time in University of Wisconsin or Wisconsin state vocational-technical and/or adult education programs; financial need; satisfactory academic standing
$ Given: Unspecified number of $1,800 awards annually; renewable to five years

WISCONSIN HIGHER EDUCATION AIDS BOARD

Wisconsin Indian Student Assistance Program
P.O. Box 7885
Madison, WI 53707
(608) 267-2206

Contact: Joyce Appel, Grant Coordinator
Restrictions: Resident of Wisconsin, one fourth or more American Indian blood of certified tribe or band; financial need; acceptance at, or eligibility for, Wisconsin institution; must be undergraduate or graduate student
$ Given: Unspecified number of awards; maximum $1,100 per year, renewable for 10 semesters of full-time study

WISCONSIN RURAL OPPORTUNITY SCHOLARSHIPS

University of Wisconsin at Platteville
1 University Plaza
Platteville, WI 53818
(608) 342-1836

Contact: Sarah Siegert
Restrictions: Wisconsin farm residents
$ Given: 10 awards of $850
Deadline: February 1

WISCONSIN TUITION GRANT PROGRAM

131 West Wilson Street, Suite 902
Madison, WI 53703
(608) 266-1954

Restrictions: Resident of Wisconsin; full-time student enrolled in college, university, or nursing school in Wisconsin which charges higher tuition than UWl-Madison; financial need
$ Given: 7,600 grants to maximum $2,172; renewable to 10 semesters

WISCONSIN VETERANS PART-TIME
Study Reimbursement Grant
Wisconsin Department of Veteran Affairs
30 West Mifflin Street
Madison, WI 53707-7843

Restrictions: Wisconsin veterans and dependents of deceased
Wisconsin veterans
$ Given: Up to $1,100

WYOMING

DODD AND DOROTHY L. BRYAN FOUNDATION
P.O. 6287
Sheridan, WY 82801
(307) 672-3535

Contact: Rose Marie Madia, manager
Restrictions: Residents of Sheridan, Campbell, and Johnson counties,
WY, and of Powder River, Rosebud, and Big Horn counties, MT, with
academic merit
$ Loaned: $4,000 per year; renewable
Deadline: June 15

ROBERT C. BYRD HONORS SCHOLARSHIP
State of Wyoming
2300 Capitol Avenue
Cheyenne, WY 82002

Contact: Dr. Jim Lendino
Restrictions: High school senior, Wyoming residents, minimum 3.8 GPA
$ Given: 14 awards of $1,500
Deadline: April 1

FFA WAL-MART SCHOLARSHIP
P.O. Box 15160
Alexandria, VA 22309-0160
(703) 360-3600

Restrictions: FFA member; freshman-year agriculture major; resident of Alabama, Arkansas, Arizona, California, Colorado, Connecticut, Delaware, Florida, Georgia, Hawaii, Idaho, Illinois, Indiana, Iowa, Kansas, Kentucky, Louisiana, Maine, Maryland, Michigan, Minnesota, Mississippi, Missouri, Montana, Nebraska, Nevada, New Hampshire, New Mexico, New York, North Carolina, North Dakota, Ohio, Oklahoma, Oregon, Pennsylvania, Puerto Rico, Rhode Island, South Carolina, South Dakota, Tennessee, Texas, Utah, Virginia, Washington State, West Virginia, Wisconsin, or Wyoming
$ Given: Approximately 50 awards of $1,000
   Deadline: February 15

PAUL STOCK FOUNDATION
1135 14th Street
P.O. Box 2020
Cody, WY 82414
(307) 587-5275

Restrictions: Wyoming residents
$ Loaned: Unspecified number of grants of approximately $2,000 each
   Deadlines: June 30, November 30

AREA OF STUDY LISTINGS

AERONAUTICS

AIR TRAFFIC CONTROL ASSOCIATION, INC.
Scholarship Awards Program
2300 Clarendon Blvd., Suite 711
Arlington, VA 22201-2302
(703) 522-5717 Fax (703) 527-7251

Contact: Gabriel A. Hartl, President
Restrictions: Full-time undergraduate or graduate students enrolled at a four-year institution in aeronautics, aviation, and related fields; U.S. citizens; grants also available to full-time ATC employees.
$ Given: Unspecified number of grants
   Deadline: August 1

AMERICAN INSTITUTE
OF AERONAUTICS AND ASTRONAUTICS
Scholarship Program
370 L'Enfant Promenade SW
Washington, DC 20024
(202) 646-7400

Contact: Patrick Gowhin
Restrictions: Student must have completed one semester at an accredited institution with a B average and be planning to enter an aerospace engineering technology field; U.S. citizens or permanent residents.
$ Given: Unspecified number of $1,000 grants; usually between 15 and 25 per year
   Deadline: January 31

AMERICAN INSTITUTE OF AERONAUTICS
AND ASTRONAUTICS UNDERGRADUATE SCHOLARSHIPS
American Institute of Aeronautics and Astronautics
1801 Alexander Bell Drive, Suite 500
Reston, VA 20191-4344
(703) 264-7500

Contact: Wil Vargas, Director of Student Programs
Restrictions: Students studying aeronautics or astronautics; freshmen not eligible; minimum 3.0 GPA
$ Given: Approximately 30 awards of $1,000
   Deadline: January 31

NATIONAL SPACE CLUB
Robert H. Goddard Space Science and Engineering Scholarship
655 15th Street Northwest, #300
Washington, DC 20005
(202) 639-4210

Restrictions: Engineering students who are college juniors planning to participate in the aerospace sciences and technologies; U.S. citizens; past research is to be demonstrated
$ Given: One $10,000 scholarship for aerospace education
   Deadline: January 10

VERTICAL FLIGHT FOUNDATION
Undergraduate/Graduate Scholarships
217 North Washington Street
Alexandria, VA 22314
(703) 684-6777

Contact: Janet Chaikin, Communications Manager
Restrictions: Students interested in pursuing careers in some aspect of helicopters or vertical flight; must be a full-time student at an accredited school of engineering; preference given to those majoring in aerospace engineering
$ Given: Eight grants of $2,000
   Deadline: February 1

WHIRLY-GIRLS SCHOLARSHIP FUND
Executive Towers 10-D
207 West Clarendon
Phoenix, AZ 85013

Contact: Charlotte Kelley
Restrictions: Awards for helicopter flight training
$ Given: Two awards of $4,500
   Deadline: November 30

ACCOUNTING

AMERICAN INSTITUTE OF CERTIFIED PUBLIC ACCOUNTANTS

Minority Scholarship Program
P.O. Box 2209
Jersey City, NJ 07303-2209
(201)575-7641
Restrictions: Black Americans, American Indians, Asians, and Hispanics to study accounting; U.S. citizens
$ Given: 400 grants up to $5,000 per academic year
   Deadline: July 1 and December 1

ARTHUR H. CARTER SCHOLARSHIP FUND

5717 Bessie Drive
Sarasota, FL 34233-2399
(941) 921-7747   Fax (941) 923-4093

Contact: Mary Cole, Office Manager
Restrictions: Students who have completed two years of accounting to pursue further undergraduate and graduate studies in accounting; formal application, including letters of recommendation and school transcripts; U.S. citizens
$ Given: 40 to 50 grants of $2,500
   Deadline: April 1

NSPA SCHOLARSHIP AWARD

1010 North Fairfax Street
Alexandria, VA 22314-1574
(703) 549-6400

Contact: Susan E. Noell
Restrictions: Accounting major; minimum 3.0 GPA
$ Given: 26 awards, range, $500–$1,000
   Deadline: March 10

SCHOLARSHIPS FOR MINORITY ACCOUNTING STUDENTS

1211 Avenue of the Americas
New York, NY 10036-8775
(212) 596 6200

Contact: Gregory Johnson
Restrictions: Afro-American, Hispanic, or Native American accounting student; minimum 3.0 GPA; academic achievement; financial need
$ Given: Awards up to $5,000
　　Deadline: July 1

AGRICULTURE

AMERICAN SOCIETY FOR ENOLOGY AND VITICULTURE SCHOLARSHIP

P.O. Box 1855
Davis, CA 95617

Restrictions: College juniors and seniors studying viticulture, enology, or any field related to the wine and grape industry; minimum 3.2 GPA
$ Given: Awards, range, $1,000–$4,000
　　Deadline: March 1

CALIFORNIA FARM BUREAU SCHOLARSHIP FOUNDATION

1601 Exposition Boulevard
Sacramento, CA 95815
(916) 924-4052

Contact: Nina Danner, Office Manager
Restrictions: California residents to study agriculture at a four-year California college or university; U.S. citizens
$ Given: 23 grants; range, $1,250–$2,000, renewable
　　Deadline: March 1

BOOKER T. WASHINGTON SCHOLARSHIPS

National FFA Foundation
P.O. Box 15160
Alexandria, VA 22309-0160
(703) 360-3600
Restrictions: Minority FFA members
$ Given: Four awards, range, $5,000–$10,000
　　Deadline: February 15

ARCHITECTURE

AIA/AIAF SCHOLARSHIP PROGRAM
American Institute of Architects Foundation
1735 New York Avenue NW
Washington, DC 20006-5292
(202) 626-7511   Fax (202) 626-7518

Contact: Mary Felber, Director
Restrictions: Students enrolled at a four-year institution in final two years of first architecture degree program accredited by the National Architectural Accrediting Board; applications may be obtained by heads of architecture departments.
$ Given: 250 grants of $2,500
    Deadline: February 1

AMERICAN INSTITUTE OF ARCHITECTS FOUNDATION
Minority Disadvantaged Scholarship Program
1735 New York Avenue NW
Washington, DC 20006-5292
(202) 626-7511   Fax (202) 626-7518

Contact: Mary Felber, Director
Restrictions: Minority and/or disadvantaged high school graduates or college freshmen to study architecture; demonstrate financial need
$ Given: 20 grants; range, $500–$3,500; renewable
    Deadline: Nomination due by December 8; application due January 15

ART

GRAPHIC ARTS TECHNICAL FOUNDATION
National Scholarship Trust Fund of the Graphic Arts
4615 Forbes Avenue
Pittsburgh, PA 15213-3796
(412) 621-6941

Contact: Ann Mayhew, Program Coordinator
Restrictions: Interest in graphic arts careers; submit SAT, PSAT/NMSQT,

or ACT score; full-time students with at least 3.0 GPA
$ Given: 250 to 300 grants of $500–$1,500 per year; renewable;
fellowships for $1,000–$3,000
        Deadlines: March 1 for high school students;
        April 1 for undergraduates

NATIONAL ASSOCIATION OF
WOMEN IN CONSTRUCTION

Undergraduate Scholarships
National Association of Women in Construction
327 South Adams Street
Fort Worth, TX 76104

Contact: Joan Mehos
Restrictions: Students studying architecture, drafting,
engineering-related technology, landscape architecture
$ Given: Approximately 50 awards of $500–$2,000
        Deadline: February 1

NATIONAL FOUNDATION FOR
ADVANCEMENT IN THE ARTS

Arts and Recognition and Talent Search
800 Brickell Avenue, Suite 500
Miami, FL 33131
(305) 377-1148   Fax (305) 377-1149

Contact: Laura Padron
Restrictions: High school seniors to study any of the creative and
performing arts; demonstrate talent; 17 or 18 by December of contest year
        $ Given: 250 to 400 grants of $100–$3,000; freshmen year only
        Deadline: October 1

NSA/ASLA STUDENT COMPETITION
IN LANDSCAPE ARCHITECTURE

1415 Elliot Place NW
Washington, DC 20007

Contact: Robert S. Brown, Jr.
Restrictions: Award is based on overall excellence of design sensitivity
to community needs, and creativity of design.
$ Given: Awards range, $500–$2,000
        Deadline: May 15

PACIFIC PRINTING AND IMAGING
ASSOCIATION

Educational Trust Scholarships
180 Nickerson, Suite 102
Seattle, WA 98109

Contact: Jim Olsen
Restrictions: Students studying printing, print management, or graphic arts technology; must live in Washington, Oregon, Arkansas, Idaho, Montana, or Hawaii
$ Given: 12 awards, range, $500–$2,500; renewable
    Deadline: April 1

SCRIPPS HOWARD FOUNDATION

Robert P. Scripps Graphic Arts Grants
P.O. Box 5380
Cincinnati, OH 45201-5380
(513) 977-3847   Fax (513) 977-3800

Contact: Scholarships Coordinator
Restrictions: Upperclassmen majoring in graphic arts for newspaper publication with potential for becoming administrators in newspaper production; U.S. citizens or legal residents
$ Given: Unspecified number of grants to $1,000–$3,000; not renewable
    Deadlines: Request application by December 20; file application by February 25

VIRGINIA MUSEUM OF
FINE ARTS FELLOWSHIP

Virginia Museum of Fine Arts
2800 Grove Avenue
Office of Education and Outreach
Richmond, VA 23221-2466
(804) 367-0824

Contact: Lee Schultz
Restrictions: One-year residents of Virginia to study art, fine arts, art history, architecture, photography, filmmaking, and video; financial need; U.S. citizens; employment experience
$ Given: 12 grants of $8,000
    Deadline: March 3

BROADCASTING

ASIAN-AMERICAN JOURNALISTS ASSOCIATION SCHOLARSHIP
Asian-American Journalists Association
1765 Sutter Street, Suite 1000
San Francisco, CA 94115
(415) 346-2051

Contact: Ms. Hien Nguyen, Program Coordinator
Restrictions: Students intent on careers in the news media;
do not have to be Asian-American; minimum 2.5 GPA; financial need
$ Given: Approximately 15 awards of $2,000
Deadline: April 15

ED BRADLEY SCHOLARSHIP
1000 Connecticut Ave. NW, Suite 615
Washington, DC 20036
(202) 467-5212

Contact: Gwen Lyda
Restrictions: Minority student who would like a career in
broadcast or cable news
$ Given: One award of $5,000
Deadline: March 1

BUSINESS

EXCEPTIONAL STUDENT FELLOWSHIP
One State Farm Plaza
SC-3
Bloomington, IL 61710
(309) 766-2039

Contact: Lynne Tammeus
Restrictions: Must be nominated by dean of college or department head.

Minimum 3.6 GPA; leadership in extracurricular activities; academic achievement, potential business administrative capacity; senior year
$ Given: 50 awards of $3,000
   Deadline: February 15

GOLDEN STATE MINORITY FOUNDATION, LB

1055 Wilshire Boulevard, Suite 1115
Los Angeles, CA 90017
(213) 482-6300 or (800) 666-4763

Contact: Ivan A. Houston, President/CEO
Restrictions: Business administration; minority upperclassmen at a California college or university; must maintain GPA of 3.0 or better; financial need; U.S. citizen or California resident
$ Given: 25 to 30 grants; range, $2,000–$2,500
   Deadline: April 1

JAMES S. KEMPER FOUNDATION, B-4

1 Kemper Drive
Long Grove, IL 60049-7164
(708) 320-2847

Restrictions: College freshmen who are business majors; must reside on campus; list of 16 participating four-year schools across the country available from the above address; must have potential to maintain 3.0 GPA
   $ Given: 15 grants of $1,500–$7,000

PRINCE GEORGE'S CHAMBER OF COMMERCE FOUNDATION SCHOLARSHIP

Prince George's Chamber of Commerce
4640 Presidents Drive, Suite 200
Lanham, MD 20706
(301) 731-5000

Contact: Robert Zinsmeister, Administrator
Restrictions: Residents of Prince George's County, MD, who have graduated from county schools; preference to business-related majors; financial need
$ Given: 17 awards annually; range, $1,000–$2,760
   Deadline: May 15

STATE FARM COMPANIES FOUNDATION
Exceptional Student Fellowship Awards
One State Farm Plaza
Bloomington, IL 61710
(309) 766-2311

Contact: Lynne Tammeus
Restrictions: Business-related fields; exceptional college juniors and seniors, nominated by dean or department head; U.S. citizen; minimum 3.4 GPA
$ Given: 50 grants of $3,000 annually
    Deadline: February 15

EDUCATION

CALIFORNIA STUDENT AID COMMISSION
Cal Grant "C" Program
P.O. Box 510845
Sacramento, CA 94245-0845
(916) 322-2807
Restrictions: California residents for minimum 12 months; undergraduates to study occupational, technical, or vocational education, or nursing; financial need; U.S. citizens; course length between 4 and 24 months
$ Given: 1,570 grants; range, $530–$2,360
    Deadline: March 2

PHI DELTA KAPPA, INC.
Scholarship Grants for Prospective Teachers
Eighth Street and Union Avenue
Bloomington, IN 47402-0789
(812) 339-1156

Contact: Howard Hill, Director of Chapter Programs
Restrictions: High school seniors in upper third of their class who plan to pursue a teaching career; based on scholastic achievement, school and community activities, recommendations, and an essay
$ Given: 43 grants; range, $1,000–$2,000
    Deadline: January 31

ENGINEERING

NATIONAL SPACE CLUB

Robert H. Goddard Space Science and Engineering Scholarship
655 15th Street NW, #300
Washington, DC 20005
(202) 639-4210

Restrictions: Engineering students who are college juniors planning to participate in the aerospace sciences and technologies; U.S. citizens; past research is to be demonstrated.
$ Given: One $10,000 scholarship
  Deadline: January 10

SOCIETY OF WOMEN ENGINEERS

General Electric Foundation Scholarships
Westinghouse Bertha Lamme Scholarships
120 Wall Street, 11th Floor
New York, NY 10005-3902
(212) 509-9577 or (800) 666-1793   Fax (212) 509-0224

Contact: Louise Bacon, Executive Assistant
Restrictions: Women to study engineering, incoming freshmen accepted at an ABET accredited engineering school; U.S. citizens or legal residents, have at least 3.5 GPA
$ Given: Unspecified number of $1,000 awards; renewable
  Deadline: May 15

SOCIETY OF WOMEN ENGINEERS

MASWE Memorial, Lillian M. Gilbreth
Ivy Parker Memorial, RCA Corporation
Grumman Corporation, Digital Equipment Scholarships
120 Wall Street, 11th Floor
New York, NY 10005-3902
(212) 509-9577 or (800) 666-1793   Fax (212) 509-0224

Contact: Louise Bacon, Executive Assistant
Restrictions: Women upper-division students who are majoring in engineering at accredited U.S. colleges and universities; minimum 3.5 GPA; financial need

$ Given: Unspecified number of grants; $2,000 (Ivy Parker); $5,000 (MASWE)

    Deadline: February 1

SOCIETY OF WOMEN ENGINEERS

Olive Lynn Salembier Scholarship
120 Wall Street, 11th Floor
New York, NY 10005-3902
(212) 509-9577 or (800) 666-1793   Fax (212) 509-0224

Contact: Louise Bacon, Executive Assistant
Restrictions: Women who have not worked as an engineer for at least two years and who wish to go to or return to school to study engineering; undergraduate or graduate; U.S. citizens
$ Given: One grant of $2,000

    Deadline: May 15

SOCIETY OF WOMEN ENGINEERS

S.W.E. Founders Scholarship
United Technologies Corporation Scholarship
Northrop Corporation Scholarship
120 Wall Street, 11th Floor
New York, NY 10005-3902
(212) 509-9577 or (800) 666-1793   Fax (212) 509-0224

Contact: Louise Bacon, Executive Assistant
Restrictions: Sophomore women majoring in engineering at accredited colleges and preparing for a B.S. degree; S.W.E. award is for student S.W.E. members, others open to non-members; have at least 3.5 GPA
$ Given: Unspecified number of $1,000 grants; renewable

    Deadline: May 15

HEALTH CARE

ADHA CERTIFICATE/ASSOCIATE DEGREE SCHOLARSHIP

444 North Michigan Avenue, Suite 3400
Chicago, IL 60611
(312) 440-8900

Restrictions: Full-time enrollment in a certificate or associate degree program leading to certification as a dental hygienist; 3.0 minimum GPA
$ Given: 25 awards of $1,000
Deadline: June 15

FOUNDATION OF NATIONAL STUDENT NURSES ASSOCIATION, INC.

555 West 57th Street, Suite 1327
New York, NY 10019
(212) 581-2211

Restrictions: Several categories of grants in different areas of nursing studies—write for information; must be enrolled in accredited nursing program; financial need; academic achievement; employment experience in community service
$ Given: 100 grants of $1,000–$2,000
Deadline: February 1

HEALTH CAREERS SCHOLARSHIP

P.O. Box 1310
Brookhaven, MS 39601

Contact: Mrs. Fred Cannon
Restrictions: Students studying nursing, medicine, dentistry, medical technology, pharmacy, occupational therapy, or physical therapy
$ Given: Approximately 50 awards, range, $500–$1,000
Deadline: April 1

NATIONAL AMBUCS SCHOLARSHIP FOR THERAPISTS

P.O. Box 5127
High Point, NC 27262
(336) 888-6052

Restrictions: Junior or senior scholarship for student study in occupational therapy, physical therapy, speech language pathology, hearing audiology, music therapy, or therapeutic recreation, minimum 3.0 GPA
$ Given: Awards range, $500–$1,500
Deadline: April 15

UNDERGRADUATE RESEARCH FELLOWSHIP IN PHARMACEUTICS

1100 15th Street
Washington, DC 20005
(202) 835-3470

Contact: Donna Moore
Restrictions: Award to encourage undergraduate students to do graduate work in pharmaceutics
$ Given: 10 awards of $5,000
    Deadline: October 1

HISTORY

DAUGHTERS OF THE AMERICAN REVOLUTION
American History Scholarship
National Society Daughters of the American Revolution
Office of the Committees Scholarships
NSDAR Administration Building
1776 D Street, NW
Washington, DC 20006-5392
(202) 879-3292

Restrictions: Graduating high school seniors in the top third of their class with at least 3.3 GPA to major in American history at U.S. institutions, financial need; U.S. citizenship; sponsorship by local DAR chapter required, send SASE to above address for application.
$ Given: Four grants; range, $1,000–$2,000 a year for four years
    Deadline: February 1

INSURANCE

SOCIETY OF ACTUARIES
Actuarial Sciences for Minority Students
475 North Martingale Road
Suite 800
Schaumberg, IL 60173-2226
(847) 706-3543   Fax (847) 706-3599

Contact: Sue Martz
Restrictions: Minority students (defined as African-American, Hispanic, Asian-American, or Native American); U.S. citizens

$ Given: 20 to 35 grants; range, $1,000–$1,200
        Deadline: May 1

JOURNALISM

DOW JONES NEWSPAPER FUND
P.O. Box 300
Princeton, NJ 08543-0300
(609) 452-2820   Fax (609) 520-5804

Contact: Jan Maressa
Restrictions: Open to college juniors, seniors, graduate students studying journalism; U.S. citizens
$ Given: 75 up to 80 paid summer internships at daily newspapers, plus scholarships of $1,000
        Deadline: November 15

NATIONAL PRESS PHOTOGRAPHERS FOUNDATION, INC.
Joseph Ehrenreich Scholarship
Detroit Free Press
321 West Lafayette Boulevard
Detroit, MI 48231
(313) 646-7286

Contact: Mike Smith
Restrictions: Career plans in photojournalism; portfolio; must have at least half year of undergraduate study remaining; financial need
$ Given: Five grants of $1,000
        Deadline: March 1

NATIONAL RIGHT TO WORK COMMITTEE
William B. Ruggles Journalism Scholarship
5211 Port Royal Road, Suite 510
Springfield, VA 22151
(703) 321-9606 ext. 238

Contact: Linda Staulcup, Public Affairs Assistant
Restrictions: Journalism, communications, advertising, and broadcasting majors; understanding of voluntarism and of the problems of compulsory unionism

$ **Given:** One $2,000 grant per year, renewable
   Deadlines: January 1, March 31

RUBEN SALAZAR SCHOLARSHIP FUND
National Association of Hispanic Journalists
1193 National Press Building
Washington, DC 20045-2100

Contact: Anna Lopez
Restrictions: Hispanic journalism students; financial need
$ **Given:** 30 awards, range, $1,000–$2,000
   Deadline: February 28

SCRIPPS HOWARD FOUNDATION
P.O. Box 5380
Cincinnati, OH 45201-5380
(513) 977-3847   Fax (513) 977-3800

Contact: Patty Cottingham, Director
Restrictions: Full-time undergraduate students with good scholastic standing and evidence of journalism proficiency, both print and broadcast; U.S. citizens; preference given to upperclassmen, prior recipients, minorities, and those living in areas of company operations; work experience requested
$ **Given:** 135 grants; range, $1,000–$3,000
   Deadline: February 25 for application request; send SASE with words "Scholarship Application"

LABOR EDUCATION

IOWA FEDERATION OF LABOR AFL-CIO
Annual Scholarship
2000 Walker Street, Suite A
Des Moines, IA 50317
(515) 262-9571

Contact: Mark Smith, Secretary-Treasurer
Restrictions: Labor education; award based on 750-word essay on the American labor movement; Iowa high school seniors only

$ Given: One grant of $1,500
     Deadline: March 30

LAW/LAW ENFORCEMENT

ASSOCIATION OF FORMER AGENTS OF THE U.S. SECRET SERVICE, INC.
J. Clifford Dietrich and Julie Y. Cross Scholarships
P.O. Box 11681
Alexandria, VA 22312

Contact: P. Hamilton Brown, Executive Secretary
Restrictions: Sophomores working toward degrees in law enforcement or police administration; U.S. citizens
$ Given: Three awards of $1,000 to $1,500 per year
     Deadline: April 30

LIBRARY SCIENCE

LOUISE GILES MINORITY SCHOLARSHIP
50 East Huron Street
Chicago, IL 60611

Restrictions: Minority library student; academic excellence
$ Given: Average award $3,000

MUSIC

ASCAP FOUNDATION GRANTS TO YOUNG COMPOSERS
1 Lincoln Plaza
New York, NY 10023
(212) 621-6327

Contact: Frances Richard

Restrictions: Composer under the age of 30
$ Given: 27 awards, range, $250–$2,500
    Deadline: March 15

CHOPIN PIANO SCHOLARSHIP

15 East 65th Street
New York, NY 10021
(212) 734-2130

Restrictions: Chopin competition; must be between the ages of 15 and 21
$ Given: Three awards of $1,000–$2,500
    Deadline: March 31

MILWAUKEE MUSIC SCHOLARSHIP

First Wisconsin Trust Company
P.O. Box 2054
Milwaukee, WI 53201
(414) 765-5123

Contact: Jewel Graff
Restrictions: Music student ages 16–26; Wisconsin resident; financial need
$ Given: Approximately four awards, range, $500–$1,000
    Deadline: February 1

MUSIC ASSISTANCE FUND SCHOLARSHIP

1156 Fifteenth Street NW, Suite 800
Washington, DC 20005-1704
(202) 776-0212

Contact: Lorri Ward
Restrictions: Afro-American attending a music conservatory; orchestral music major planning a career with a symphony orchestra
$ Given: 55 awards, range, $500–$2,500
    Deadline: December 15

EMILY K. RAND SCHOLARSHIP

92 Raymond Road
Brunswick, ME 04011
(207) 725-1125

Contact: Joyce Chaplin
Restrictions: Cumberland, Oxford, or York county resident between the ages of 17 and 25

$ Given.   Four awards, range, $500–$1,200
    Deadline: May 6

PERFORMING ARTS

ARTS RECOGNITION AND TALENT SEARCH
800 Brickell Avenue, Suite 500
Miami, FL 33131
(800) 970-ARTS

Contact: Laura Padron, Program Coordinator
Restrictions: High school senior pursuing dance, classical, jazz, theater, visual arts, photography, or creative writing
$ Given: 400 awards, range, $100–$3,000
    Deadline: October 1, June 1

POLITICAL SCIENCE

NATIONAL SOCIETY DAUGHTERS
OF THE AMERICAN REVOLUTION
Office of the Committees: Scholarships
Enid Hall Griswold Memorial Scholarship
1776 D Street, NW
Washington, DC 20006-5392
(202) 879-3292

Contact: Cindy Rummell, Administrative Assistant
Restrictions: Political science/government/history/economics students; upperclassmen attending accredited U.S. institutions; U.S. citizens; minimum 3.0 GPA; apply through local DAR chapter; financial need
$ Given: One to three $1,000 grants
    Deadline: February 15

HARRY S TRUMAN SCHOLARSHIP
712 Jackson Place NW
Washington, DC 20006
(202) 395-4831

Restrictions: Senior award for student in top quarter of class with leadership potential planning to go to graduate school to prepare for a career in public service
$ Given: 85 awards, range, $3,000–$13,500
    Deadline: January 23

UNITED STATES SENATE YOUTH PROGRAM

90 New Montgomery Street, Suite 1212
San Francisco, CA 94105-4504
(800) 841-7048

Contact: Rita A. Almon, Program Director
Restrictions: High school junior or senior; student body member; leadership ability
$ Given: $2,000
    Deadline: Late September or October

WASHINGTON CROSSING FOUNDATION SCHOLARSHIP

P.O. Box 17
Washington Crossing, PA 18977-0017
(215) 493-6577

Contact: Dr. Walter W. Robson III
Restrictions: High school seniors planning a career in government service; 200-word essay on reasons for choosing career in government service with reference to inspirational aspect of George Washington's crossing the Delaware; U.S. citizens; academic achievement; age: 20 or under
$ Given: One of $10,000, one of $7,500, three of $2,500 each, and other grants as funding allows; also, unspecified number of grants in varying amounts available to students residing in the 13 original states
    Deadline: January 15 or next business day

SCIENCE

ACS MINORITY SCHOLARSHIP

1155 16th Street NW
Washington, DC 20036
(202) 872-6250

Contact: Dorothy Rodmann, Scholarship Administrator
Restrictions: Chemistry majors
$ Given: Approximately 200 awards, range, $2,500–$5,000
   Deadline: February 1

AMERICAN GEOLOGICAL INSTITUTE

Minority Participation Program Scholarships
4220 King Street
Alexandria, VA 22302-1502
(703) 379-2480

Contact: Marilyn Suitor, Director, Education and Human Resources
Restrictions: Full-time minority students in the geosciences, or high school seniors intending to study geosciences; 3.0 GPA; U.S. citizens
$ Given: 90 grants; range, $500–$10,000
   Deadline: February 1

SEG FOUNDATION SCHOLARSHIP

P.O. Box 702740
Tulsa, OK 74170-2740
(918) 497-5500

Contact: Marge Gerhart, Scholarship Coordinator
Restrictions: Students pursuing a career in exploration geophysics; academic achievement
$ Given: 80 awards, range, $500–$3,000
   Deadline: March 1

SIGMA XI GRANTS-IN-AID OF RESEARCH

99 Alexander Drive
Research Triangle Park, NC 27709

Restrictions: Students inclined toward careers as science investigators
$ Given: Awards range, $100–$2,500
   Deadline: February 1, May 1, November 1

MISCELLANEOUS LISTINGS

AIR FORCE SERGEANTS ASSOCIATION SCHOLARSHIP
P.O. Box 50
Temple Hills, MD 20757-0050

Restrictions: Unmarried, under 23, dependent of an AFSA member; academic ability
$ Given: Grants range, $2,000–$5,000
    Deadline: April 15

CARGILL SCHOLARSHIP FOR RURAL AMERICA
Cargill Inc.
P.O. Box 15160
Alexandria, VA 22309-0160
(703) 360-3600

Contact: Gladys Tripp
Restrictions: High school seniors from farm families; U.S. citizens; for students enrolling for two to four years in vocational schools, universities, and colleges; financial need
$ Given: 250 awards of $1,000 each
    Deadline: February 15

EDUCATIONAL COMMUNICATIONS SCHOLARSHIP FOUNDATION
P.O. Box 5002
Lake Forest, IL 60045 5002
(708) 295-6650

Contact: Judy Casey, Assistant to the Chairman
Restrictions: High school seniors and college students throughout the U.S.; awards based on merit; 3.0 GPA; age: 20 or under; U.S. citizens; financial need
$ Given: 175 grants; average $1,000
    Deadline: May 31

ELKS NATIONAL FOUNDATION
Most Valuable Student Award
2750 Lake View Avenue
Chicago, IL 60614-1889
(312) 929-2100

Contact: A. Patricia Kavanaugh, Executive Director
Restrictions: U.S. citizens living within jurisdiction of B.P.O. Elks of the USA; top 5% rank in high school class; financial need, leadership, and scholastic achievement; age: 20 or under
$ Given: 500 scholarships for $1,000–$5,000 per year for four years
   Deadline: January 15

NATIONAL ASSOCIATION OF
PLUMBING-HEATING-COOLING CONTRACTORS
NAPHCC Scholarship Program
P.O. Box 6808
Falls Church, VA 22046-1148
(703) 237-8100

Contact: Kelly Carson, Scholarship Liaison
Restrictions: Sponsorship by a member in good standing of the NAPHCC for at least one year; high school seniors and incoming freshmen enrolled in B.A. programs to study business administration, engineering, or construction; U.S. citizens only
$ Given: Three grants of $2,500; renewable
   Deadline: April 1

NATIONAL HONOR SOCIETY SCHOLARSHIP
National Association of Secondary School Principals
1904 Association Drive
Reston, VA 22091
(703) 860-0200

Contact: National Honor Society adviser, local chapter
Restrictions: High school seniors nominated by their local National Honor Society chapters, based on scholarship, leadership, character, and service
$ Given: 250 awards for $1,000 each
   Deadline: February 3

HATTIE M. STRONG FOUNDATION

1620 I Street, NW, Suite 700
Washington, DC 20006
(202) 331-1619

Contact: Robin Tanner
Restrictions: Juniors at accredited four-year colleges
$ Loaned: 280 loans; range, up to $3,000
   Deadline: March 31

PHI KAPPA THETA NATIONAL FOUNDATION

3901 West 86th Street, Suite 425
Indianapolis, IN 46268
(317) 872-9034

Contact: Scott Bora
Restrictions: Members of Phi Kappa Theta fraternity
$ Given: Five to eight grants; range, $300–$1,500
   Deadline: April 30

LEOPOLD SCHEPP FOUNDATION

551 Fifth Avenue, Suite 3000
New York, NY 10176-2597

Contact: Mrs. Edythe Bobrow, Executive Secretary
Restrictions: Undergraduate and graduate students, enrolled full-time at accredited colleges and universities; academic achievement and financial need; U.S. citizens; must mail a SASE with inquiry
$ Loaned: 150 to 200 grants; range, $1,000–$7,500
   Deadline: November 1

SPENCE REESE FOUNDATION

Boys and Girls Clubs of San Diego
3760 Fourth Avenue, No. 1
San Diego, CA 92103
(619) 298-3520

Contact: John W. Treiber, President/CEO
Restrictions: High school male students majoring in medicine, law, engineering, or political science; preference is given to those living within a 250-mile radius of San Diego. Send SASE for application.

$ **Given:** Four grants of $2,000
 Deadline: May 15; initial approach by letter stating academic achievements and educational goals

TYSON FOUNDATION, INC.

2210 West Oak Lawn
Springdale, AR 72762-6999
(501) 290-4955   Fax (501) 290-7984

Contact: Cheryl J. Tyson, Manager
Restrictions: Students attending accredited colleges and universities and majoring in agriculture, business, computer science, engineering, or nursing, residing in vicinity of Tyson's Center; U.S. citizens or permanent residents
$ **Given:** 100 grants; range, $400–$1,200
 Deadline: April 15

GRANTS FOR WOMEN

AMERICAN FOUNDATION FOR THE BLIND

R. L. Gillette Scholarship Fund
11 Penn Plaza, Suite 300
New York, NY 10001
(212) 502-7662

Contact: Julie Tucker
Restrictions: Legally blind women to study literature or music, attending a four-year institution; recommendation from high school and/or college advisor and a one-page personal statement of career objectives and goals; U.S. citizens
$ Given: Two grants for $1,000 each
  Deadline: April 1

EXECUTIVE WOMEN INTERNATIONAL SCHOLARSHIP PROGRAM

Executive Women International
515 South 700 East, Suite 2E
Salt Lake City, UT 84102
(801) 355-2800

Contact: Debra G. Tucker
Restrictions: Freshmen-year scholarship for women studying business or any professional field of study which requires a four-year degree
$ Given: 130 awards, range, $50–$10,000
  Deadline: March 1

JEWISH FOUNDATION FOR EDUCATION OF WOMEN SCHOLARSHIP

330 West 58th Street
New York, NY 10019
(212) 265-2565

Contact: Florence Wallach, Executive Director
Restrictions: Full-time students who live within a 50-mile radius of New

York City (including New Jersey and Long Island)
$ Given: Annual awards, range, $500–$3,500
    Deadline: January 31 for coming year

NEVADA WOMEN'S FUND

P.O. Box 50428
Reno, NV 89513
(702) 786-2335

Contact: Fritsi H. Ericson
Restrictions: Female Nevada residents
$ Given: Approximately 50 awards, range, $500–$5,000
    Deadline: March 1

SOCIETY OF WOMEN ENGINEERS

General Electric Foundation Scholarships
Westinghouse Bertha Lamme Scholarships
120 Wall Street, 11th Floor
New York, NY 10005-3902
(212) 509-9577 or (800) 666-1793 Fax (212) 509-0224

Contact: Louise Bacon, Executive Assistant
Restrictions: Women to study engineering, incoming freshmen accepted at an ABET accredited engineering school; U.S. citizens or legal residents
$ Given: Unspecified number of $1,000 awards; renewable
    Deadline: May 15

SOCIETY OF WOMEN ENGINEERS

MASWE Memorial, Lillian M. Gilbreth
Ivy Parker Memorial, RCA Corporation
Grumman Corporation, Digital Equipment Scholarships
120 Wall Street, 11th Floor
New York, NY 10005-3902
(212) 509-9577 or (800) 666-1793 Fax (212) 509-0224

Contact: Louise Bacon, Executive Assistant
Restrictions: Women upper-division students who are majoring in engineering at accredited U.S. colleges and universities; minimum 3.5 GPA; financial need
$ Given: Unspecified number of grants; $2,000 (Ivy Parker); $5,000 (MASWE)
    Deadline: February 1

GRANTS FOR ETHNIC STUDENTS

AMERICAN GEOLOGICAL INSTITUTE
Minority Participation Program Scholarships
4220 King Street
Alexandria, VA 22302-1502
(703) 379-2480

Contact: Marilyn Suitor, Director, Education and Human Resources
Restrictions: Full-time minority students in the geosciences, or high school seniors intending to study geosciences; 3.0 GPA; U.S. citizens
$ Given: 90 grants; range, $500–$10,000; $7,000 for undergraduates, $4,000 for graduate students
Deadline: January 31

AMERICAN INSTITUTE OF CERTIFIED PUBLIC ACCOUNTANTS
Minority Scholarship Program
P.O. Box 2209
Jersey City, NJ 07303-2209
(212) 596-6200

Restrictions: Black Americans, American Indians, Asians, and Hispanic undergraduates to major in accounting; graduate students may study taxation, finance, or business administration
$ Given: 210 grants to $5,000 per year
Deadline: July 1

AMERICAN INSTITUTE OF POLISH CULTURE, INC.
1440 79th Causeway, Suite 117
Miami, FL 33141
(305) 864-2349

Contact: Mr. Fred Martin, Chairman
Restrictions: Young Americans of Polish descent to study journalism/public relations

$ Given: Two grants of $2,500 each
   Deadline: January 15

ARMENIAN STUDENT'S ASSOCIATION SCHOLARSHIP

Armenian Student's Association of America, Inc.
395 Concord Avenue
Belmont, MA 02178

Contact: Christine Williamson
Restrictions: Students of Armenian ancestry; financial need; academic performance; extracurricular involvement; attend full-time an accredited institution
$ Given: 30 to 50 grants; range, $500–$2,500
   Deadline: March 15

CHINESE PROFESSIONAL CLUB OF HOUSTON SCHOLARSHIP

11302 Fallbrook Drive
Houston, TX 77065
(713) 955-0115

Contact: James Tang, M.D. Scholarship Committee Chairman
Restrictions: Residents of Houston, TX, metropolitan area who are individuals of Chinese descent
$ Given: Eight awards; range, $600–$1,500
   Deadline: November 15

GOLDEN STATE MINORITY FOUNDATION

1055 Wilshire Boulevard, Suite 1115
Los Angeles, CA 90017
(213) 482-6300 or (800) 666-4763

Contact: Ivan A. Houston, President/CEO
Restrictions: Business administration, economics, or related fields; minority upperclassman at a California college or university; must maintain at least 3.0 GPA; financial need; U.S. citizen or legal resident
$ Given: 25 to 30 grants; range, $2000–$2,500
   Deadline: April 1

JOSE MARTI SCHOLARSHIP CHALLENGE

Florida Department of Education
Office of Student Financial Assistance
Florida Education Center, Room 1344

Tallahassee, FL 32399-0400
(904) 487-3260

Restrictions: U.S. citizens residing in and attending college or university full time in Florida; must be Hispanic or of Spanish culture, e.g., Mexico, South America, Central America, or the Caribbean; financial need; minimum 3.0 GPA; Florida residency
$ Given: Each grant $2,000, renewable
Deadline: May 15

NAACP ROY WILKINS SCHOLARSHIP
NAACP Youth and College Division
4805 Mount Hope Drive
Baltimore, MD 21215-3297
(410) 358-8900

Contact: Andrea E. Moss, Education Department
Restrictions: High school seniors with minority background; active NAACP members preferred; financial need; leadership qualities; minimum 2.5 GPA
$ Given: 20 awards; range, $500–$1,000
Deadline: April 30

PELLEGRINI SCHOLARSHIP FUND
Swiss Benevolent Society of New York
37 West 67th Street
New York, NY 10023
(212) 246-0655

Restrictions: Students of Swiss descent (one parent must be a Swiss national).
$ Given: Awards range from $500 to $3,000
Deadline: March 31

SCRIPPS HOWARD FOUNDATION
P.O. Box 5380
Cincinnati, OH 45201-5380
(513) 977-3847   Fax (513) 977-3800

Contact: Patty Cottingham, Director
Restrictions: Full-time undergraduate or graduate students with good scholastic standing and evidence of journalism proficiency, both print and

broadcast; preference given to upperclassmen, prior recipients, minorities, and those living in areas of company operations; work experience requested
$ Given: 135 grants; range, $1,000–$3,000
Deadline: February 25 for application request; send only a self-addressed mailing label with words "Scholarship Application"

SEMINOLE-MICCOSUKEE INDIAN SCHOLARSHIP PROGRAM

Florida Department of Education
Office of Student Financial Assistance
255 Collins
Florida Education Center, Room 1344
Tallahassee, FL 32399-0400
(904) 487-0049

Contact: Appropriate tribal office:

* Miccosukee Tribe of Florida
c/o Higher Education Committee/Billy Cypress, President
P.O. Box 440021
Tamiami Station
Miami, FL 33144

* Seminole Tribe of Florida
c/o Higher Education Committee/Pat Jagiel,
Asst. Director of Education
6073 Sterling Road
Hollywood, FL 33024

Restrictions: Seminole and Miccosukee Indians enrolled in eligible Florida colleges/universities; financial need
$ Given: Based on need

UNITED NEGRO COLLEGE FUND

Scholarship Program
500 East 62nd Street
New York, NY 10021
(212) 326-1100

Contact: Educational Services Department
Restrictions: Students enrolled at United Negro College Fund member

institutions; financial need; minimum 2.5 GPA, plus other college-specific criteria
$ Given: Over 1,000 grants; range, $750–$7,500
  Deadline: None

WASIE FOUNDATION SCHOLARSHIP

Wasie Foundation
U.S. Bank Place, Suite 4700
601 Second Avenue South
Minneapolis, MN 55402
(612) 332-3883

Contact: Lea Johnson, Scholarship Administrator
Restrictions: Christian students of Polish ancestry attending full-time specified Minnesota institutions; financial need; academic ability; extracurricular activities; personal qualities; members of the Communist Party not eligible
$ Given: 50 awards; range, $500–$3,500
  Deadline: April 15

GRANTS FOR DISABLED STUDENTS

AMERICAN COUNCIL OF THE BLIND SCHOLARSHIP

American Council of the Blind
1155 15th Street NW, Suite 720
Washington, DC 20005
(202) 467-5081   Fax (202) 467-5085

Contact: Jessica Beach, Assistant Scholarship Coordinator
Restrictions: Legally blind U.S. citizens or resident aliens accepted into postsecondary programs; several award categories; students with 3.3. GPA generally given preference
$ Given: 25 grants; range, $500–$4,000
   Deadline: March 1

AMERICAN FOUNDATION FOR THE BLIND

R. L. Gillette Scholarship Fund
11 Penn Plaza, Suite 300
New York, NY 10001
(212) 502-7600 or (212) 502-7662

Contact: Julie Tucker
Restrictions: Legally blind women enrolled in a four-year literature or music program; recommendation from high school and/or college advisor and a one-page personal statement of career objectives and goals; U.S. citizens
$ Given: Two grants of $1,000 each
   Deadline: April 1

ALEXANDER GRAHAM BELL ASSOCIATION FOR THE DEAF

Robert H. Weitbrecht Scholarship Award
3417 Volta Place NW
Washington, DC 20007-2778
(202) 337-5220

Contact: Virginia Gilmer
Restrictions: Oral deaf students, born with profound impairment or having suffered such impairment before acquiring language, accepted into full-time academic program for hearing students; North American citizens; to study engineering or science
$ Given: 65 grants; range, $250–$1,000; renewable once
  Deadline: April 1

STANLEY E. JACKSON, SCHOLARSHIP FOR THE HANDICAPPED
Foundation for Exceptional Children
1920 Association Drive
Reston, VA 22091
(703) 620-1054

Contact: Kenneth Collins
Restrictions: Disabled incoming freshmen enrolling full-time in undergraduate or vocational training programs; one award specified for members of ethnic minority groups
$ Given: Four grants; range, $500–$1,000
  Deadline: February 1

LIGHTHOUSE CAREER INCENTIVE AWARDS PROGRAM
800 Second Avenue
New York, NY 10017
(212) 808-0077

Contact: Gilda Gold
Restrictions: Legally blind student residing in New England, New York, New Jersey, or Pennsylvania; financial need not a criteria
$ Given: Approximately five awards averaging $5,000
  Deadline: January 31

NATIONAL FEDERATION OF THE BLIND
Scholarship Committee
814 Fourth Avenue, Suite 200
Grinnell, IA 50112
(515) 236-3366

Contact   Peggy Pinder Elliott, Chairman of the Scholarship Committee
Restrictions: Must be legally blind and pursuing (or planning to pursue) a full-time postsecondary course of study. Eleven scholarships (refer to list below) with additional restrictions as noted; all awarded on the basis of

academic excellence, service to the community, and financial need
$ Given: Refer to list below
> **Deadline:** March 31 for all scholarships

NATIONAL FEDERATION OF THE BLIND SCHOLARSHIPS LIST:

American Action Fund Scholarship, one award of $10,000, no additional restrictions

National Federation of the Blind Scholarships, 16 grants of $3,000 to $4,000; no additional restrictions

Melva T. Owen Memorial Scholarship, one award of $4,000; study must be directed toward attaining financial independence; excludes religious study and study that is meant only to further general or cultural education.

Howard Brown Richard Scholarship, one award of $3,000; preference given to those studying architecture or engineering

National Federation of the Blind Humanities Scholarship; one award of $3,000; winner must be studying in the traditional humanities such as art, English, foreign languages, history, philosophy, or religion.

National Federation of the Blind Educator of Tomorrow Award, one award of $3,000; winner must be planning a career in elementary, secondary, or postsecondary education.

Hermione Grant Calhoun Scholarship, one award of $3,000; winner must be a woman; 2.5 GPA minimum.

Kuchler-Killian Memorial Scholarship, one award of $3,000, no additional restrictions; 3.5 GPA

BIBLIOGRAPHY

John Bear, *Bear's Guide to Finding Money for College.* Berkeley, Calif.: Ten Speed Press, 1993.

Laurie Blum, *Free Money for Foreign Study.* New York: Facts On File, 1992.

Daniel J. Cassidy, *The Scholarship Book: The Complete Guide to Private Sector Scholarships.* Englewood Cliffs, N.J.: Prentice Hall Trade, 1996.

The College Blue Book: Scholarships, Fellowships, Grants, and Loans. Englewood Cliffs, N.J.: Prentice-Hall, 1995.

Victoria L. Hall, *Foundation Grants to Individuals,* 10th ed. New York: Foundation Center, 1997.

Elizabeth Olson, *Education Dollars for College: The Quick Guide to Financial Aid for Engineering.* Garrett Park, Md.: Garrett Park Press, 1997.

Gail A. Schlachter, *College Student's Guide to Merit and Other No-Need Funding.* San Carlos, Calif.: Reference Service Press, 1996–1998.

———. *How to Find out about Financial Aid: A Guide to over 700 Directories Listing Scholarships, Loans, Grants, Awards, and Internships.* San Carlos, Calif.: Reference Service Press, 1995–97.

Scholarships and Loans for Nursing Education. New York: National League for Nursing, 1994.

John Schwartz, *College Scholarships and Financing.* Englewood Cliffs, N.J.: Prentice Hall & IBD, 1997.

W. Wickremasinghe, *Scholarships & Grants for Study or Research in USA: A Scholarship Handbook.* Houston, Tex.: American Collegiate Service, 1996.

Erlene B. Wilson, *Money for College: A Guide to Financial Aid for African-American Students.* New York: Plume, 1996.

INDEX

A

Abe and Annie Seibel Foundation, The, 145

Abilene Christian University Leadership Awards, 139

Academic Scholars Program (Oklahoma), 117

accounting, 171–72

Achievement Awards (Oregon), 119

ACS Minority Scholarship, 188–89

Adams Scholarship Fund, 64

ADHA Certificate/Associate Degree Scholarship, 180–81

aeronautics, 169–71

African-American students, 10, 16, 42, 122, 126, 147, 172, 186. *See also* minorities

agriculture, 9, 117, 172

AIA/AIAF Scholarship Program, 173

Aid for Public College Students Grants Program, 17

Air Force Sergeants Association Scholarship, 191

Air Traffic Control Association, Inc., 169

Alabama, 1–3

Alabama GI Dependents' Scholarship Program, Department of Veterans Affairs, 1

Alaska, 3–4

Alexander Graham Bell Association for the Deaf, 203–4

Alexander Scholarship Fund, Thomas L., Myrtle R., Arch and Eva, 39

Almanor Scholarship Fund, 7

Amarillo Area Foundation, Inc., 140

American Council of the Blind Scholarship, 203

American Foundation for the Blind, 195, 203

American Geological Institute, 189, 197

American Indian Endowed Scholarship, 154

American Institute of Aeronautics and Astronautics, 169

American Institute of Aeronautics and Astronautics Undergraduate Scholarships, 170

American Institute of Architects Foundation, 173

American Institute of Certified Public Accountants, 171

American Institute of Polish Culture, Inc., 197

American Legion
Auxiliary Department of Iowa, 44
Department of Michigan, 69
Department of New Hampshire, 87
Department of Wisconsin, 162
National High School, 108

American Legion Oratorical Contest
Pennsylvania, 124
Tennessee, 137–38

American Legion Robert E. David Scholarship for the Children of Vietnam and Korean War Veterans, 131

American Society for Enology and Viticulture Scholarship, 172

Anna and Charles Stockwitz Fund for Education of Jewish Children, 14

Anna M. Vincent Trust, 128

Ann Arbor Area Community Foundation, 69

Annis I. Fowler/Kaden Scholarship, 135

Ann Lane Scholarship, 142–143

application process, viii–ix

architecture, 145, 173, 175

Arizona, 4

Arkansas, 5–7

Arkansas Single Parent Sholarships, 5

Arkansas Student Assistance Grant Program, 5

Armenian Student's Association Scholarship, 198

art, 17, 62, 117, 173–75

Arthur H. Carter Scholarship Fund, 171

Arts Recognition and Talent Search, 187

ASCAP Foundation Grants to Young Composers, 185–86

Asian-American Journalists Association Scholarship, 176

Association of Former Agents of the U.S. Secret Service, Inc., 185

athletic scholarships, xi, 58

Avon Products, Inc., 110–11

Awards of Excellence (Washington State), 155

B

Bagley Scholarship, Marion J., 87

Bair Memorial Trust, Charles M., 82

Baker Education Fund, Jessie H., 94

Bamberger Memorial Foundation, Ruth Eleanor and John Ernest, 148

Barnes Scholarship Trust, Fay T., 140

Barnett Memorial Scholarship, Marguerite Ross, 79

Barrington Educational Fund, Richard and Jessie, 85–86

Barr Scholarship, Walter S., 64

Barth Foundation, Inc., The Theodore H., 64

Baruch Scholarships, 94–95

basketball, 63

Bell Association for the Deaf, Alexander Graham, 203–4

Bennett Memorial Corporation, The James Gordon, 95

Bernard Dany Educational Fund, 120

Blanche and Thomas Hope Fund
Kentucky, 52
Ohio, 112

Blazek Foundation, Joseph, 32

Board of Trustees Academic Awards (Louisiana), 54

Boettcher Foundation Scholarships, 15

Bogardus Trust, Katherine, 32

Borrego Springs Educational Scholarship Committee, 7

Bour Memorial Scholarship Trust, 79

Bowen Foundation, Inc., Ethel N.
Virginia, 152
West Virginia, 158

Boynton Gillespie Memorial Fund, 34

Boy Scouts, 34, 39, 57, 65, 87, 93, 129, 150

Bradley Scholarship, Ed, 176

Brandeis University Community
Service Award, 65

Brey Memorial Endowment Fund,
Claude and Ina, 48

broadcasting, 176

Brown Trust, Gabriel J., 108

Bruce L. Crary Foundation, Inc.,96

Bruce McMillan Jr. Foundation, Inc.,
143

Bryan Collegiate Students Fund, Fred
A., 39

Bryan Foundation, Dodd and
Dorothy L.
Montana, 82
Wyoming, 167

Buckeley Scholarship Fund, Leonard
H., 17

Buffalo Foundation, The, 95

Bunn Memorial Fund, Henry, 33

Burgess Memorial Scholarship Fund,
The William, Agnes & Elizabeth,33

Burkett Trust, George W., 39–40

Burton Foundation, The William
T. and Ethel Lewis, 54

Bushee Foundation, Inc., Florence
Evans, 65

business, 46, 176–78

Byrd Honors Scholarship, Robert C.
Delaware, 20
Florida, 22
Georgia, 25
Indiana, 40
Missouri, 79
North Carolina, 104
Oregon, 120
South Dakota, 134-135
Texas, 140
Wyoming, 167

C

Cal Grant 8

California, 7–14

California Farm Bureau
Scholarship Foundation, 172

California Student Aid
Commission, 8, 178

California Teachers Association, 8–9

Callaway Foundation, Fuller E., 25

Cal State B, 8

Cameron Educational Foundation,
The Dave, 131

Camp Foundation, 152

Cape Foundation, Inc., 25-26

Career Advancement Awards
(New Jersey), 89

Cargill Scholarship for Rural
America, 191

Carman Scholarship Trust, Nellie
Martin, 155

Carolina Scholars Finalist Awards,131

Carter Scholarship Fund, Arthur H.,
171

Carter Trust Boy Scout Scholarship,
Marjorie Sells
Maine, 57-58
Massachusetts, 65
New Hampshire, 87-88
Rhode Island, 129
Vermont, 149-150

C.G. Fuller Foundation, 132

Charles A. Winans Memorial Trust,
14

Charles E. Saak Trust, 13

Charles M. Bair Memorial Trust, 82

Chautauqua Region Community
Foundation, Inc., 95

chemistry, 32, 145

Cherokee Nation of Oklahoma, 117

Chet Jordan Leadership Award, 58

Cheyenne-Arapaho Tribal Scholarship, 117–118

Chinese Professional Club of Houston Scholarship, 140–141, 198

Chopin Piano Scholarship, 186

Christian A. Herter Memorial Scholarship, 66-67

C.K. Eddy Family Memorial Fund, 69–70

C.L. Rowan Charitable and Educational Fund, Inc., 144

Clara Stewart Watson Foundation, 148

Clark Foundation Scholarship Office, 95–96

Claude and Ina Brey Memorial Endowment Fund, 48

Clem Jaunich Education Trust, 74–75

Cole Foundation, Inc., Olive B., 40

Colgan Fund, The James W., 65–66

Collins-McDonald Trust Fund, 120

Colorado, 15–17

Colorado Masons Benevolent Fund Association, The, 16–17

Colorado State University, 15

Colorado Undergraduate Merit Award, 15

Connecticut, 17–20

Connecticut Independent College Student Grant Program, 18

Corti Family Agricultural Fund, The, 9

Crary Foundation, Inc., Bruce L., 96

Culver Community High School, 41

D

Dane G. Hansen Foundation, 49

Dany Educational Fund, Bernard, 120

Daughters of the American Revolution, 182

Dave Cameron Educational Foundation, The, 131

David and Eula Winterman Foundation, The, 148

David Wasserman Scholarship Fund, Inc., 103–4

Davis Foundation, Inc., James A. and Juliet L.

Kansas, 48

Missouri, 79–80

D.D. Hachar Charitable Trust Fund, 141

Delaware, 20–21

Delaware Higher Education Commission, 20

Delegate Scholarship (Maryland), 60

Department of New Hampshire Scholarship, 88

Department President's Scholarship, 111

Direct Student loans, x

District of Columbia, 22

District of Columbia State Student Incentive Grant, 22

Dodd and Dorothy L. Bryan Foundation

Montana, 82

Wyoming, 167

Douglas Teacher Scholarship, Paul Louisiana, 55

Maryland, 61
Montana, 82
North Dakota, 108
Tennessee, 137–138
Virginia, 152
West Virginia, 159
Dow Jones Newspaper Fund, 183

E

Easter Seal Society of Iowa, Inc., 44–45
Ebell of L.A. Scholarship Endowment Fund, and the Mrs. Charles N. Flint Scholarship Endowment Fund, The, 9
Ed Bradley Scholarship, 176
Eddy Family Memorial Fund, C.K., 69–70
Ed E. and Gladys Hurley Foundation
Arkansas, 6
Louisiana, 55–56
Texas, 142
education, 178. *See also* teaching
education, labor, 184–85
Educational Assistance Grant, 61
Educational Communications Scholarship Foundation, 191
Educational Opportunity Grant, 155–156
Educational Opportunity Program, 96
Edward Bangs and Elza Kelley Foundation, Inc., 67
Edward Ruthledge Charity, 164
Edwards Scholarship Fund, 66
Edwin L. and Louis B. McCallay

Educational Trust Fund, 113
Edwin T. Meredith Foundation. *See* Meredith Foundation, Edwin T.
Memorial Scholarship Foundation, 41
ELKS National Foundation, 192
Ella G. McKee Foundation, 37
Elmer O. and Ida Preston Educational Trust, 47
El Paso Community Foundation, The, 141
Emily K. Rand Scholarship, 59–60, 186–87
employee tuition benefits, x
engineering, 32, 145, 157, 179–80
Ethel N. Bowen Foundation, Inc.
Virginia, 152
West Virginia, 158
ethnic students, 197–201
Ewald Foundation, H.L., 70
Exceptional Student Fellowship, 176–77
Executive Women International Scholarship Program, 195

F

Fahrney Education Foundation, 45
Fannie & John Hertz Foundation, 11
Faught Memorial Scholarships, 150
Fay T. Barnes Scholarship Trust, 140
federal aid, ix–x
Federal Direct Student loans, x
Federal Perkins loans, ix
Federal Plus loans, x
Federal Stafford loans, x

Federal Work-Study, ix

FFA Wal-Mart Scholarship, 1. *See also specific state*

Field Cooperative Association, Inc., 77

Fields Trust, Laura, 118

Florence Evans Bushee Foundation, Inc., 65

Florida, 22–25

Florida Department of Education, 23, 23–24

Florida Leader Magazine, 24

Florida Postsecondary Student Assistance Grant, 24

Florida Private Student Assistance Grant, 24

Ford Educational Foundation Inc., Guy Stanton, 162

Ford Family Foundation Scholarship, 121

Ford Fund, The S.N. and Ada, 112

foreign students, 26

Forsythe Educational Trust Fund, Fred, 58

Foundation for the Carolinas, 104–105

Foundation of National Student Nurses Association, Inc., 181

Fowler/Kaden Scholarship, Annis I., 135

Fowler Memorial Scholarship, Paul L.

Idaho, 30

Washington State, 156

Franklin Lindsay Student Aid Fund, 143

Frank Roswell Fuller Scholarship, 18

Fred A. Bryan Collegiate Students Fund, 39

Fred B. and Ruth B. Zigler Foundation, 57

Fred Forsythe Educational Trust Fund, 58

Friendship Fund, Inc., 66

FSEOG (Federal Supplemental Educational Opportunity Grants), ix

Fukunaga Scholarship Foundation, 29

Fuller E. Callaway Foundation, 25

Fuller Foundation, C.G., 132

Fuller Scholarship, Frank Roswell, 18

G

G. William Klemstine Foundation, 125

Gabriel J. Brown Trust, 108

George and Mary Josephine Hamman Foundation, 142

George E. Stifel Scholarship Fund, 160

George J. Record School Foundation, 116

George T. Welch Testamentary Trust, 158

George W. and Sadie Marie Juhl Scholarship Fund, 71

George W. Burkett Trust, 39–40

Georgia, 25–28

Georgia Student Finance Authority, 27

Georgia Tuition Equalization Grant, 27

Gibson Foundation, 1

Gibson Foundation, Addison H., 124

Gilbert Grant, 66

Giles Minority Scholarship, Louise, 185

Gillespie Memorial Fund,Boynton, 34

Golden Gate Restaurant Association, 10

Golden State Minority Foundation, 198

Golden State Minority Foundation, LB, 177

Golden State Minority Foundation Scholarship, 10

Goldstein Scottish Rite Trust, 3

Governor's Scholars, 6

Graham-Fancher Scholarship Fund, 11

Grand Haven Area Community Foundation, Inc., 70–71

Grand Rapids Foundation, 71

grant applications, viii–ix

grants, federal, ix

Graphic Arts Technical Foundation, 173–74

Greater Kanawha Valley Foundation, The, 159

Griffin Educational Fund, Abbie M., 88

Guaranteed Access Grant Program (Maryland), 62

guidelines, viii

Guy Stanton Ford Educational Foundation Inc., 162

H

Hachar Charitable Trust Fund, D.D., 141

Haines Memorial Scholarship, 135

Hamman Foundation, George and Mary Josephine, 142

handicapped students, 53, 203–5

Hansen Foundation, Dane G., 49

Harless Foundation, Inc., James, 160

Harold and Sara Wetherbee Foundation, 28

Harris and Eliza Kempner Fund, 142

Harry S Truman Scholarship, 187–88

Hattie M. Strong Foundation, 193

Hauss-Helms Foundation, Inc., 112

Hawaii, 28–30

health care, 1, 6, 71, 90, 145, 148, 157, 180–82. *See also* nursing

Health Careers Scholarship, 181

Helvering Trust, R.L. and Elso, 49

Henry Bunn Memorial Fund, 33

Henry E. and Florence W. Snayberger Memorial Foundation, 128

Herschel C. Price Educational Foundation, 160

Herter Memorial Scholarship, Christian A., 66–67

Hertz Foundation, Fannie & John, 11

Higher Education Opportunity Program Grant, 97

Hispanic students, 10, 25, 42, 122, 147, 172. *See also* minorities

history, 146, 175, 182

Hodges Fund, Mary E., 130

Hoffman Scholarship Trust, James M., 2

Hope Fund, Blanche and Thomas
Kentucky, 52
Ohio, 112

Hope Grant Program, 27

Horace Smith Fund, 68

hotel management, 10

House Educational Trust, Susan Cook, 33

H.T. Ewald Foundation, 70

Humboldt Area Foundation, The, 11

Hurley Foundation, Ed E. and Gladys
Arkansas, 6
Louisiana, 55–56
Texas, 142

I

Idaho, 30–32

Ilgenfritz Testamentary Trust, May
H., 80

Illinois, 32–38

Illinois Department of the
American Legion Scholarships, 34

Illinois Department of the American
Legion Scouting Scholarships,
34–35

Illinois Educational Opportunities
for Children of Veterans, 35

Illinois Student Assistance
Commission, 35, 36

Indiana, 39–44

Indiana Nursing Scholarship Fund,
41-42

insurance, 182–83

Iowa, 44–47

Iowa College Student Aid
Commission, 45–46

Iowa Federation of Labor AFL-CIO,
184–85

Iowa Grants, 46

J

Jack Shinin Memorial Scholarship,
122–123

Jackson, Scholarship for the
Handicapped, Stanley E., 204

Jackson & White, Student Aid Fund,
Maria C. and General George A.,
123

Jacob Stump Jr. & Clara Stump
Memorial Scholarship Fund, 38

James A. and Juliet L. Davis
Foundation, Inc.

Kansas, 48

Missouri, 79–80

James F. Mulholland Scholarship,
97–98

James Harless Foundation, Inc., 160

James Lee Love Scholarships, 105

James M. Hoffman Scholarship
Trust, 2

James S. Kemper Foundation, B-4,
177

James W. Colgan Fund, The, 65–66

James Z. Naurison Scholarship Fund

Connecticut, 19

Massachusetts, 68

Janesville Foundation, Inc., 163

Jaunich Education Trust, Clem,
74–75

J.C. Stewart Memorial Trust, 63–64

Jenson American Legion, Maynard,
84

Jerome B. Steinbach Scholarship, 123

Jessie H. Baker Education Fund, 94

Jewell Memorial Foundation, The
Daniel Ashley & Irene Houston, 28

Jewish Foundation for Education of
Women Scholarship, 89–90, 97,
195–96

Jewish students, 9, 14, 36, 90, 97,
195–96

J.F. Maddox Foundation, 93

John B. and Brownie Young
Memorial Fund, 54

John M. Will Memorial Scholarship
Foundation, 78

John McIntire Educational Fund, 113

John W. and Rose E. Watson
Foundation, 73–74

John W. Will Journalism
Scholarship, 2–3

Jones Foundation, The Harvey and
Bernice, 6

Jordan Leadership Award, Chet, 58

Jose Marti Scholarship, 25

Jose Marti Scholarship Challenge, 198–99

Joseph Blazek Foundation, 32

journalism, 2–3, 12, 78, 133, 144, 183–84

Juhl Scholarship Fund, George W. and Sadie Marie, 71

Junior Miss Award (Mississippi), 77

K

Kansas, 48–51

Kansas Board of Regents, 49, 49–50

Kansas Commission of Veterans' Affairs Scholarships, 50

Kansas Minority Scholarship Program, 50

Kansas Nursing Scholarship Program, 50

Kansas Teacher Scholarship Program, 51

Katherine Bogardus Trust, 33

KCPQ-TV-Ewing C. Kelly Scholarship, 156–157

Kelley Foundation, Inc., Edward Bangs and Elza, 67

Kemper Foundation, B-4, James S., 177

Kempner Fund, Harris and Eliza, 142

Kent Medical Foundation, 71

Kent State University, 112–113

Kentucky, 51–54

Kentucky Center for Veterans Affairs Benefits For Veterans and Their Dependents, 52

Kentucky Department of Education, 52–53

Kentucky Tuition Grant, 53

Klemstine Foundation, G.

William, 125

Kohler Foundation, Inc., 163

L

labor education, 184–85

La Crosse Community Foundation, 163

Lane Scholarship, Ann, 142–43

Laura E. Porter Trust, 51

Laura Fields Trust, 118

Law Enforcement Officers and Fireman, 78

law/law enforcement, 185

Lawrence Lutterman Memorial Scholarship, 90

Leonard H. Buckeley Scholarship Fund, 17–18

Leopold Schepp Foundation, The, 102, 193

Lesher Foundation Scholarship, Margaret and Irvin, 125

letter, viii

Levie Educational Fund, Marcus & Theresa, 36

library science, 185

Lighthouse Career Incentive Awards Program, 204

Lindsay Student Aid Fund, Franklin, 143

loans, ix–x

Loats Foundation, 62

Louise Giles Minority Scholarship, 185

Louisiana, 54–57

Louisiana Office of Student Financial Assistance, 56

Louisville Community Foundation, Inc., The, 53

Love Scholarships, James Lee, 105

Lutterman Memorial Scholarship, Lawrence, 90

M

Maddox Foundation, J.F., 93

Maine, 57–60

Maine Community Foundation, Inc., The, 59

Maine Student Incentive Scholarship, 59

Maine Students Incentive Scholarship Program, 59

Maloney Foundation, William E., 67

Marcus & Theresa Levie Educational Fund, 36

Margaret and Irvin Lesher Foundation Scholarship, 125

Marguerite Ross Barnett Memorial Scholarship, 79

Maria C. Jackson—General George A. White, Student Aid Fund, 123

Marion J. Bagley Scholarship, 87

Marjorie Sells Carter Trust Boy Scout Scholarship. See Carter Trust Boy Scout Scholarship, Marjorie Sells

Mark and Catherine Winkler Foundation, 154

Marti Scholarship, Jose, 25

Marti Scholarship Challenge, Jose, 198–99

Mary E. Hodges Fund, 130

Mary K. and Edith Pillsbury Foundation, 12

Maryland, 60–64

Maryland State Scholarship Administration, 62, 62–63

Massachusetts, 64–69

Massachusetts Office of Student Financial Assistance, 67, 67–68

Massachusetts State Scholarship

Program Office of Student Financial Assistance, 68

May H. Ilgenfritz Testamentary Trust, 80

Maynard Jenson American Legion, 84

McCallay Educational Trust Fund, Edwin L. and Louis B., 113

McCurdy Memorial Scholarship Foundation, 72

McFarland Charitable Foundation, 36–37

McIntire Educational Fund, John, 113

McKee Foundation, Ella G., 37

McMillan Jr. Foundation, Inc., Bruce, 143

McWherter Scholars Program, Ned, 138

medicine. See health care

Meredith Foundation, Edwin T.
Illinois, 37
Indiana, 42
Iowa, 47
Kansas, 51
Michigan, 72
Minnesota, 75
Missouri, 80–81
Nebraska, 84
New York, 97
North Dakota, 109
Ohio, 113
Oklahoma, 118–19
Pennsylvania, 125
South Dakota, 136
Wisconsin, 163

Meriden Foundation, The, 19

Mesa State College, 16

Michigan, 69–74

Michigan Adult Part-time Grants, 72

Michigan Department of Education, 72–73, 73

Michigan Educational Opportunity Grant, 73

Middlesex County Medical Society Foundation, Inc., 90

Milwaukee Music Scholarship, 164, 186

Minear Educational Trust, Ruth M., 42

Minnesota, 74–76

Minnesota Higher Education Coordinating Board, 75

Minnesota Higher Education Services Office, 75

minorities, 10, 50, 53, 89, 101, 106, 113, 138, 145, 154, 173, 176, 177, 182, 185, 197–201

Minority Teacher and Special Education Services Scholarship, 42

minority teachers, 37, 42, 52–53, 138–139

Minority Teachers of Illinois Scholarship, 37

Minority Teaching Fellows Program, 138

Mississippi, 77–78

Missouri, 79–81

Missouri Coordinating Board for Higher Education, 81

Missouri Teacher Education Scholarship, 81

M.L. Shanor Foundation, The, 145

Montana, 82–83

Moody Foundation, The, 143

Mower Memorial Scholarship, Barbara Alice, 29

Mulholland Scholarship, James F., 97–98

music, 12, 102, 117, 164, 185–87

Music Assistance Fund Scholarship, 186

Muskegon County Community Foundation, Inc., 73

N

NAACP Roy Wilkins Scholarship, 199

National Ambucs Scholarship for Therapists, 181

National Association of Plumbing-Heating-Cooling Contractors, 192

National Association of Women in Construction, 174

National Basketball Association, 63

National Federation of the Blind, 204–5

National Foundation for Advancement in the Arts, 174

National Honor Society Scholarship, 192

National Press Photographers Foundation, Inc., 183

National Right to Work Committee, 183–84

National Society Daughters of the American Revolution, 187

National Space Club, 170, 179

Native American students, 10, 23, 103, 109, 118, 122, 155, 166, 172. *See also* minorities

Naurison Scholarship Fund, James Z.

Connecticut, 19

Massachusetts, 68

Navy

Connecticut, 19

New Jersey, 92

New York, 98

Nebraska, 84–85

Nebraska Scholarship Assistance Program, 85

Nebraska State Scholarship Award Program, 85

Ned McWherter Scholars Program, 138

Need Grant Program (Washington State), 157

Negro Educational Emergency Drive, 125–126

Nellie Martin Carman Scholarship Trust, 155

Nevada, 85–87

Nevada Student Incentive Grant Program, 86

Nevada Women's Fund, 196

New Hampshire, 87–89

New Hampshire Charitable Fund, 89

New Hampshire Incentive Program, 89

New Jersey, 89–92

New Jersey Department of Higher Education, 90–91

New Mexico, 92–94

New Mexico Military Institute, 93

New Mexico Veterans' Service Commission, 93–94

New Orphan Asylum Scholarship Foundation, 114

New York, 94–104

New York Aid for Part-time Study, 98

New York Council Navy League Scholarship, 19, 98

New York Council Navy League Scholarship Fund, 92

New York State Higher Education Services Corporation, 98

Niccum Educational Trust Foundation, 43

North Carolina, 104–7

North Carolina Association of Insurance Agents Scholarship, 105

North Carolina Division of Veterans Affairs, 105–6

North Carolina Freshmen Scholars Program, 106

North Carolina State Assistance Authority, 106

North Carolina Teaching Fellows Program, 106

North Dakota, 108–10

North Dakota Indian Scholarship Program, 109

North Dakota Scholars Program, 109

North Dakota State Grant Program, 110

North Dakota Student Financial Assistance Grants, 110

Northern Kentucky University, 53–54

Northern New York Community Foundation, 100

NSA/ASLA Student Competition in Landscape Architecture, 174

NSPA Scholarship Award, 171

Nucor Foundation, Inc.
Alabama, 2
Arizona, 4
Indiana, 43
Nebraska, 85
North Carolina, 106–7
South Carolina, 132
Texas, 143-144
Utah, 149

nursing, 37, 42, 46, 50, 71, 90, 178, 181

O

Oakland Scottish Rite Scholarship Foundation, 11–12

Ohio, 110–17

Ohio Student Aid Commission, 114–15

Ohio Student Loan Commission, 115

Ohio War Orphans Scholarship Board, 115

Oklahoma, 117–19

Oklahoma Tuition Aid Grant, 119

Olin Scott Fund, Inc., 150

Olive B. Cole Foundation, Inc., 40

Oppenheim Students Fund, Inc., 101

Oratorical Contest Scholarship
  Iowa, 47
  Virginia, 153
  Wisconsin, 164

Oratorical Contest Scholarships (Texas), 144

Oregon, 119–23

Oregon AFL-CIO ASAT-MAY Darling Scholarship, 121

Oregon Department of Veterans' Affairs, 121

Oregon Need Grant, 122

Oregon PTA, 122

Oshkosh Foundation, 164

P

Pacific Gas and Electric Company, 12

Pacific Printing and Imaging Association, 175
  Arkansas, 6–7
  Hawaii, 29–30
  Idaho, 31
  Montana, 83
  Oregon, 122
  Washington State, 157

Palmetto Fellows Scholarship, 132–33

Parrett Scholarship Trust Fund, Arthur and Doreen, 157–58

Part-time Student Instructional Grant Program (Ohio), 115

Paul Douglas Teacher Scholarship. *See* Douglas Teacher Scholarship, Paul

Paul L. Fowler Memorial Scholarship
  Idaho, 30–31
  Washington State, 156

Paul Stock Foundation, 168

Pellegrini Scholarship Fund, 199

Pellerin Foundation, Willis and Mildred, 56–57

Pell grants, ix

Pennsylvania, 124–29

Pennsylvania Department of Military Affairs, 126

Pennsylvania Higher Education Assistance Agency, 126–27

performing arts, 187

Perkins loans, ix

Perry S. and Stella H. Tracy Scholarship Fund, 14

Phi Delta Kappa, Inc., 178

Phi Kappa Theta National Foundation, 193

physics, 32, 145

Pillsbury Foundation, Mary K. and Edith, 12

political science, 187–88

Porter Trust, Laura E., 51

Potlatch Foundation for Higher Education Scholarship
  Arkansas, 7
  California, 12–13
  Idaho, 31
  Minnesota, 76
  Nevada, 86–87

Press Club of Dallas Foundation Scholarships, 144

Preston Educational Trust, Elmer O. and Ida, 47

Price Educational Foundation, Herschel C., 160

Prince George's Chamber of Commerce Foundation Scholarship, 63, 177

Pritchard Educational Fund, 47

proposals, viii

Q

Quaker Chemical Foundation, 127

R

Ratner, Miller, Shafran Foundation, The, 115–16

Rebekah Scholarship Award, 38

Record School Foundation, George J., 116

Reese Foundation, Spence, 193–94

references, viii–ix

Rhode Island, 129–30

Rhode Island Higher Education Assistance Authority, 130

Richard and Jessie Barrington Educational Fund, 85–86

Richland County Foundation of Mansfield, Ohio, The, 116

R.L. and Elso Helvering Trust, 49

Robert C. Byrd Honors Scholarship. See Byrd Honors Scholarship, Robert C.

Robert C. Thomas Memorial Scholarship Loan Fund, 3–4

Robert Schreck Memorial Educational Fund, 144–45

Rochester Institute of Technology, 101

Roothbert Fund, Inc., 101

Rowan Charitable and Educational Fund, Inc., C.L., 144

Ruben Salazar Scholarship Fund, 184

Ruth Eleanor and John Ernest Bamberger Memorial Foundation, 148

Ruthledge Charity, Edward, 164

Ruth M. Minear Educational Trust, 42

S

Saak Trust, Charles E., 13

Sachs Foundation, 16

Scalp and Blade Scholarship Trust, 101–2

Schepp Foundation, The Leopold, 102, 193

Scholarship Foundation of Santa Barbara, 13

Scholarship Fund, Inc. (Ohio), 116

Scholarship Incentive Program (Delaware), 21

Scholarships for Minority Accounting Students, 172

Scholastic Achievement Grant Program (Connecticut), 19–20

Schreck Memorial Educational Fund, Robert, 144–45

science, 17, 32, 157, 188–89

Scripps Howard Foundation, 175, 184, 199–200

Searls Scholarship Fund, William, 60

SEG Foundation Scholarship, 189

Seibel Foundation, The Abe and Annie, 145

Seminole-Miccosukee Indian Scholarship Program, 200

Shannon Scholarship, 127

Shanor Foundation, The M.L., 145

Sharpe Memorial Scholarship, Thomas C., 102

Shinin Memorial Scholarship, Jack, 122–23

Sico Foundation

Delaware, 21

Pennsylvania, 127

Sigma XI Grants-in-aid of Research, 189

Simpson Foundation, The, 2

single parents, 5, 115, 154

Skidmore College, 103

Smith Fund, Horace, 68–69

S.N. Ford and Ada Ford Fund, The 112

Snayberger Memorial Foundation, Henry E. and Florence W., 128

Society of Actuaries, 182–83

Society of Women Engineers, 179–80, 196

South Carolina, 131–34

South Carolina Department of Veterans Affairs, 133

South Carolina Press Association Foundation Newspaper Scholarship, 133–34

South Carolina State Student Incentive Grant, 134

South Carolina Teacher Loan and South Carolina Governor's Teaching Scholarship Loan, 134

South Carolina Tuition Grants Commission, 134

South Dakota, 134–37

South Dakota Department of Education and Cultural Affairs, 136

South Dakota Division of Veterans Affairs, 136–37

Spence Reese Foundation, 193–94

Sprint/Carolina Telephone Scholarship Program, 107

Stafford loans, federal, x

Stanley E. Jackson, Scholarship for the Handicapped, 204

State Aid to Native Americans, 103

State Educational Incentive Grant Program, 3

State Farm Companies Foundation, 178

State of Idaho Scholarship, 31

State Scholarship Program for Ethnic Recruitment (Texas), 145–46

State Student Assistance Commission of Indiana, 43–44

State Student Assistance Commission of Indiana Higher Education Awards, 43

State Student Incentive Grant

Mississippi, 78

Texas, 146

Steinbach Scholarship, Jerome B., 123

Stephenson Scholarship Foundation, 13

Stewart Memorial Trust, J.C., 63–64

Stifel Scholarship Fund, George E., 160

Stockwitz Fund for Education of Jewish Children, Anna and Charles, 11

Stonecutter Foundation, Inc., 107

Stony-Wold Herbert Fund, Inc., 103

Strong Foundation, Hattie M., 193

Student Aid Foundation (Georgia), 28

Stump Memorial Scholarship Fund, Jacob Stump Jr. & Clara, 38

Sunnyside, Inc., 146

Susan Cook House Educational Trust, 33

Swiss Benevolent Society of Chicago, The, 38

T

Talent Incentive Program, 165

teaching, 51, 103, 106, 134, 160, 178. *See also* Douglas Teacher Scholarship, Paul minority teachers, 37, 42, 53, 138–39

Tennessee, 137–39

Tennessee Student Assistance Corporation, 139

Texas, 140–48

Texas History Essay Contest, 146

Texas Public Educational Grant, 146–47

theology, 145

Thomas C. Sharpe Memorial Scholarship, 102

Thomas L., Myrtle R., Arch and Eva Alexander Scholarship Fund, 39

Thomas Memorial Scholarship Loan Fund, Robert C., 3–4

Tozer Foundation, Inc., 76

Tracy Scholarship Fund, Perry S. and Stella H., 14

Treacy Company
  Idaho, 32
  Montana, 83
  North Dakota, 110
  South Dakota, 137

Truman Scholarship, Harry S, 187–88

Tuition Aid for Needy Students Program (Connecticut), 20

Tuition Equalization Grant (Texas), 147

Twenty-first Century Scholars Award (Indiana), 44

Ty Cobb Educational Foundation, 26

Tyson Foundation, Inc., 194

U

Undergraduate Research Fellowship in Pharmaceutics, 181–82

Underwood-Smith Teacher Scholarship Program, 160

United Federation of Teachers, 103

United Negro College Fund, 200–1

United States Senate Youth Program, 188

University of Colorado/Boulder, 17

University of Tennessee, Knoxville, 139

University of Vermont Scholarships, 150

Urann Foundation, 69

USL Foundation Scholarships, 57

Utah, 148–49

UTD Presidential, 147

V

Van Wert County Foundation, The, 117

Vermont, 149-151

Vermont Part-time Student Grants, 151

Vermont Student Assistance Corporation, 151

Vertical Flight Foundation, 170

veterans, xi, 1, 35, 44, 50, 52, 60, 69, 84, 94, 99, 105, 111, 115, 121, 123, 131, 133, 136, 148, 165, 167

Veterans and Dependents Tuition Exemption, 147–48

Veterans Dependents Educational Benefits, 60

veterinary medicine, 145

Viles Foundation, Inc., 94

Vincent Trust, Anna M., 128

Virginia, 152–54

Virginia Museum of Fine Arts Fellowship, 175

Virginia State Council of Higher Education, 153–54, 154

Vivienne Camp Scholarship, 9

W

Walter S. Barr Scholarship, 64

Washington Crossing Foundation Scholarship, 188

Washington Post, 22

Washington Scholars, 158

Washington Scholarships, Booker T., 172

Washington State, 155–58

Wasie Foundation Scholarship, 76–77, 201

Wasserman Scholarship Fund, Inc., David, 103–4

Watson Foundation, Clara Stewart, 148

Watson Foundation, John W. and Rose E., 73–74

Welch Testamentary Trust, George T., 158

Weston Family Scholarship, 123

West Virginia, 158–61

West Virginia Higher Education Foundation, 161

West Virginia Italian Heritage Festival Scholarship, 161

West Virginia State College and University Systems, 161

Wetherbee Foundation, Harold and Sara, 28

Whirly-Girls Scholarship Fund, 170–71

William, Agnes & Elizabeth Burgess Memorial Scholarship Fund, The, 33

William E. Maloney Foundation, 67

William F. Winter Teacher Scholar Loan Program, 78

William P. Willis Scholarship, 119

William Searls Scholarship Fund, 60

Williams (Frank P. and Clara R.) Scholarship, 128

William T. and Ethel Lewis Burton Foundation, The, 54

Willis and Mildred Pellerin Foundation, 56–57

Willis Scholarship, William P., 119

Will Journalism Scholarship, John W., 2–3

Will Memorial Scholarship Foundation, John M., 78

Winans Memorial Trust, Charles A., 14

Windham Foundation, The, 151

Winkler Foundation, Mark and Catherine, 154

Winship Memorial Scholarship Foundation, 74

Winston-Salem Foundation, The, 107

Winterman Foundation, The David and Eula, 148

Winter Teacher Scholar Loan Program, William F., 78

Wisconsin, 162–67

Wisconsin Academic Excellence Scholarship, 165

Wisconsin Department of Veteran Affairs, 165

Wisconsin Higher Education Aids Board, 165–66

Wisconsin Rural Opportunity Scholarships, 166

Wisconsin Tuition Grant Program, 166

Wisconsin Veterans Part-time, 167

Wolf Foundation, Benjamin and Fedora, 128–29

women, 17, 28, 29, 89, 179, 195–96

Work-Study, federal, ix

Wyoming, 167–68

Y

Young Memorial Fund, John B. and Brownie, 54

Z

Zigler Foundation, Fred B. and Ruth B., 57